How to Survive
Your 40th Birthday

How to Survive Your 40th Birthday

Bill Dodds

Illustrations by
Dave Allen

 **Meadowbrook Press**

Distributed by Simon & Schuster
New York

Library of Congress Cataloging-in-Publication Data

Dodds, Bill
  How to survive your 40th birthday.
    p. cm.
    1. Middle age – Humor. 2. Forty (The number) –
Psychological aspects. 3. Middle age – Psychological aspects.
I. Title. II. Title: How to survive your fortieth birthday.
PN6231.M47D6   1990   818'.5402—dc20   90-36859
                                                   CIP

ISBN: 0-88166-139-2

Editor: Bruce Lansky
Production Editor: Clara Jeffery
Art Director: Kevin Bowen
Production Manager: David Garbe
Illustrator: Dave Allen
Cover Illustrator: Dave Allen

Simon & Schuster Order # 0-671-72561-0

Published by Meadowbrook Press, 5451 Smetana Drive,
Minnetonka, MN 55343

BOOK TRADE DISTRIBUTION by Simon & Schuster, a division
of Simon and Schuster, Inc., 1230 Avenue of the Americas,
New York, NY 10020.

01   14

Printed in the United States of America.

For Mary and Mike, the big kids, always first,
including the first to turn 40.
And for Teresa and Betsy, the little girls, who no longer
mind being the youngest in the family.

Contents

Life After 40

Is there life after 40? Yes. But don't get your hopes up. Remember that you didn't have much of a life *before* 40. People who love you very dearly will want to tease you about your birthday. They'll say funny things like:

- Ha ha ha! Now you are really old and you haven't done *squat* with your life!

And:

- You'd better make out your will soon or you'll up and die and Uncle Sam will inherit all your money.

Don't let them bother you. Once you survive your 40th birthday – and please notice that we didn't say *celebrate* your 40th birthday – you'll know you can survive almost any major trauma.

A Word or Two to Cheap Friends and Relatives

No, not to our cheap friends and relatives. To yours.

If you're looking for a reasonably priced gift for that special someone who's hitting The Big Four-O, we highly recommend a copy of *How to Survive Your 40th Birthday*. This book doesn't cost much more than a birthday card, and you can claim you slipped a $20 bill in here that the birthday boy or girl *must* have thrown out with all the wrapping paper.

Twenty dollars? Shoot! You can say you stuck 50 bucks in here. We'll never tell.

Chapter One

What Is 40?

So you're turning 40. The Big Four-O. The first thing you ought to realize is that it isn't the end of the world. The world – with its Swiss-cheese ozone layer, 30-weight-oil beaches, green-house effect, acid rain, war, famine, pestilence, and plague – is doing just fine.

Especially compared to you. You're a *real* mess.

No doubt you've noticed that your family, friends, co-workers, acquaintances, and people on the street have been saying you're "almost 40" since the day you turned 39. Hey, remember how Jack Benny always said he was 39? You do? That's a very bad sign. Young people don't even know who he was. So here's lesson one: When someone says, "Hey, you're as old as Jack Benny," you answer, "Jack who?"

Is 40 a Lot?

It will help you a great deal to keep in mind that 40 isn't necessarily a lot.

Say, for example, you're 40 pounds overweight.

Or 40 members of your spouse's family are coming to spend the weekend.

Or you're 40 miles from the nearest gas station and your tank is empty and your kid's bladder is full.

Hey, what's the big deal, right?

That's What Friends Are For

It's the people around you who will try to turn your 40th birthday into a big deal. The younger people want to lord it over you because you act like such a big shot most of the time just because you're older. They sense this is their chance to *really stick it to you!* They are the ones who keep the "Happy Birthday" black balloon business thriving.

The older people just smile and shake their heads, as if they know something you don't. And if they told you, you wouldn't believe it. You can handle all this if you just keep in mind that there's more to life after 40. Old age and death.

"Avoid the Problem, Dahling!"

The only way to avoid all this is to *never turn* 30. As soon as you turn 30, you're "almost 40." But obviously, it's too late for you! While you were still in your 20s you could have killed yourself or become a Gabor sister. (We hesitate to bring this up because, given those choices, it certainly sounds like we're advocating suicide.)

It will help if you remember that you used to think 25 was old. A *quarter of a century*. Wow, man! 'Bout time to finish getting that degree, huh? Do yourself a favor and, before your birthday, hang around with some 25-year-olds. Do you really want to be one of *them*?

Just Plain 40

The problem is no one turns "just 40." Or 30. Or 50. Any birthday with a zero in it means trouble. People say "The Big Four-O" just to watch you wince. It's more socially acceptable than hitting you over the head with a hammer, and much more effective.

You need to practice hearing those words. Stand in front of the bathroom mirror and say "Four-o, four-o, four-o, four-o..." until the phrase has no more meaning than a politician saying, "I won't raise taxes," or your child saying, "I did my homework." Remember how much fun you used to have as a kid saying one or two words over and over again until they had no meaning? You do? Uh oh.

It's a bad sign if you can remember any game that didn't need batteries or a computer chip.

Twenty-four Little Hours

There's a lot of hype that surrounds turning 40, but, really, what's the big deal? You're only 24 hours older than you were the day before. Of course, if you figure 24 hours times 365 days times 40 years plus a little more for ten February 29ths, why, you're talking.... So don't figure it out that way.

Be honest. You've already felt "old," haven't you? When that kid at the supermarket said, "Can I carry those bags to the car for you, ma'am?" Or that fine-looking woman on the bus – the one you winked at as you held your stomach in – stood up and said, "Here, sir. You sit down."

Am I Old?

Are you old? Only you can say for sure. You still might not be a geezer, a duffer, a frump, or a hag, but you could be well on your way. Here's a simple quiz to help you find out.

1. A fun evening is:
    A. "Dallas" and an ice cream bar. But not one with chocolate because sometimes the caffeine keeps me awake for hours after the show is over.
    B. Getting drunk, waking up in a strange place, and trying to discover the location of my new tattoo.

2. I like to eat:
    A. Salads and herb tea.
    B. Rat burgers, greaseball fries, and draft beer.

3. The most important thing in my life is:
    A. Making the minimum payments on my major credit cards.
    B. Rat burgers, greaseball fries, draft beer, getting drunk, waking up in strange places, and trying to discover the location of my new tattoo.

4. My car is:
    A. A station wagon.
    B. Hell on wheels.

5. What our country needs is:
    A. A tax break for middle-income families.
    B. See 2B.

There's no need to score this. You were right. You're old.

Famous People Under 40

One advantage of turning 40 is that you can quit reading those stupid lists of Famous People Who Did Famous Things While They Were Very Young (translation: Just What in the Hell Have You Accomplished with Your Life, Jack?).

You know, things like:

- Mozart wrote a bunch of music and died.

- Chuck Lindbergh flew to France.

- Bon Jovi's latest album went platinum. (We were going to say, "Tiffany's album went gold," but we were afraid you would get confused and think we were talking about the jewelry store and lose your train of thought, so we didn't. Instead we put "Bon Jovi." We sure hope you didn't confuse them with "Bon Ami" but, hey, we can't spoon-feed you, so, come on, try to keep up, OK?)

- Some jock just out of college signed a contract with a major league team and makes more in half a game than you'll make in your entire life. (Which, by the way, is *half over*.)

Anyway, you used to be able to read lists like this and say, "Yeah, someday I'll accomplish something when I'm young and I'll be on these lists."

Wrong again.

Famous People Over 40

There are very, very many famous people over 40. They are either dead or look like they are under 40. A lot of them are movie and TV stars. They are on commercials saying, "I don't mind being over 40 because I look like I'm under 40. I don't mind being over 40 because I'm not you. Buy this brand of farm implement. It's the best. It's what I use when I'm out plowing. Honest."

Get it?

No, not the tractor. Get the point? All famous people are either *under* 40 or *over* 40. Nobody who actually *is* 40 ever accomplished *anything*. Get ready to take a year off. You've earned it.

"So," you might be asking just about now, "turning 40 isn't all that bad?"

Turning 40 is easy. You don't have to do anything to accomplish that except not die. The hard part is surviving all the hoopla that surrounds turning 40.

The Big Four-O

The problem is that turning 40 isn't the only sign that you're getting older. But you wouldn't have even noticed the other signs if everyone around you wasn't laughing and pointing and saying (in a very nasal way), "Na-na-na-na-naaaa, you're turning 40. Ha-ha-ha-ha-ha-haaaa." To avoid these people you've crawled back in bed and pulled the covers up over your head and wept uncontrollably for several days. Good plan.

So let's talk about sex. There. See? You aren't dead. We'll talk about that later. We promise. And we'll discuss your boss and your old classmates and gingivitis and how you want to buy an Alfa Romeo and all sorts of other things you'd like to do. Those are just a part of what 40 is all about. But, unfortunately, so is your surprise party.

Oops! No, there's no party. (Wink, wink.) You said you don't want one so nobody is going to give you one. (Wink.) But on your birthday would you mind spending from 5 to 7 P.M. out in the garage with a Sony Walkman in your ears and an empty weed-and-feed bag over your head? Come on. Just do it. And then…would you mind coming into the living room for just a minute? Because…um, the sofa is on fire. *Really*!

OK, everybody, get down, get down, get down, SHHHHHH!, here comes….

Chapter Two

The Surprise Party

On your birthday you will be escorted into your living room, where you will see a lot of fat people trying to hide behind small pieces of furniture. They will pop out and yell, "SURPRISE!" You reply, "Oh, what a surprise. My, my, my."

MEMORIZE THAT LINE! If you don't, you just might blurt out what you really mean, "Get out of my house and leave me alone!"

The Theme Party

A 40th birthday party is more than just a mob of people sucking up free drinks and chowing down free food at your expense. It *is* that, of course, but it's much, much more. All those people have agreed to come by to see for whom the bell tolls and to help yank the rope.

Unless the people around you are very creative, your party's theme will most likely be:

- Nursing home.

- Old folks' home.

- Funeral home.

- Cemetery.

Join in the merriment. Smile broadly, laugh heartily, and say, "This is really wonderful. Not only do I get to have a lot of strangers invade my home on a day when I feel particularly vulnerable, but they also force me to ridicule people who are ill or elderly or deceased."

Party hearty.

Here are some handy one-liners to help you be a *big hit* at your party, no matter which theme is chosen.

Nursing home: "Speaking of nursing, that's what I plan to do to an extremely large bottle of scotch for the rest of the evening."

Old folks' home: "Now I know I'm over the hill. Here I am in an old folks' home and I feel peer pressure."

Funeral home: "Where'd you get that organ player, Yankee Stadium? Ta-ta-ta-Tut-ta-Ta! Charge!"

Cemetery: "You know, pardners, as long as you're planting me on Boot Hill, I sure as hell hope somebody got me *that lousy, stinking BB gun I've wanted since I was nine and not some lousy, stinking, dumb-butt gag gifts!*"

His & Hers

We don't want sexism to rear its ugly head here, but perhaps you didn't want a BB gun; perhaps you wanted a Barbie doll.

One that wasn't a hand-me-down from an older sister who had given it a Cyndi Lauper haircut. (Cyndi Lauper is a singer who sometimes sports a waffle cut. Never mind.) And you didn't get both of Barbie's shoes because your brother stuck one way up his nose and as far as anyone can tell it's still there. And you, by God, loved Barbie's little shoes. (Did you know these days Barbie wears a pair of tiny running shoes and carries her pointy-toed spikes in her purse so she can change once she gets to the office?) In any case, feel free to substitute "Barbie doll" for "BB gun."

Yeah, yeah, yeah, you never wanted one of those. Right. We believe you. Liar. You know what happened to Pinocchio. Better be careful. Now that you're getting old, your nose and ears are going to be getting bigger anyway. (No, they don't really grow. Your head shrinks.)

Good Taste and Good Fun

Where did your family and friends get the idea for your party's theme? They went to a joke and puzzle store that specializes in plastic vomit, imitation doggie doo-doo, whoopee cushions, and a wide assortment of humiliating gifts for people turning 40. Did you notice how the black-bordered napkins match the black balloons?

And One to Grow On

"What about a birthday spanking?" you ask.

There. See? Time hasn't straightened out all the coils in the King or Queen of Kink, has it? Here we are discussing a nice birthday party and you want to talk about *sex*.

Why would the author even allow such a thing to happen? Why not just ignore your wandering, filthy mind? Mainly because, if you were just skimming this, you just hit the brakes. Pretty neat, huh? Don't believe it?

Sex! There you go again. Whoa, fasten your seat belt.

The Guest List

Speaking of birthday parties and sex, people of both sexes will probably be at your party, but that's all right because your mother will be there to chaperon. If you think *you* feel old, what about her? She has a *kid* who's turning 40.

Be sure to take some time to look around the room and ask yourself, "Who are all these old people blowing up these stupid balloons?" They're your younger brothers and sisters, that's who. Being helped by your spouse and kids. And then there's that Very Large Neighbor who can smell free alcohol up to three miles away. And some people from work you don't like. And your trusty old dog who has no control over his bowels.

Who are these people? Why are they here? Why are you here? What's the meaning of life? What should you do with the time you have left on this planet? Is there an afterlife? You better sit down. BUT NOT IN THAT CHAIR!

"HA HA!" says your Very Large Neighbor. "We knew we'd get you sooner or later."

You found the whoopee cushion.

Beware of Geeks Bearing Gifts

Now that you're finally sitting in the chair reserved for the guest of honor, it's time to open presents. Don't you wish the invitation had read, "Your presents are requested?" It didn't. It said, "Bring gag gift." Get ready to gag.

All your gifts will fall into three basic categories:

1. Items that old people need.

2. Things that old people need.

3. Stuff that old people need.

No BB gun. No Barbie doll. What can you say?

You might be speechless. But if you just sit there and whimper, people will say, "You're not being a Good Sport." It is very, very important to be a Good Sport at your 40th birthday party. So here's what you'll get and here's what you say:

- Hemorrhoid cream: "Oh, goody. Wrinkle remover."

- Denture cream: "Oh, goody. Chopper stopper. I just hope I don't get it mixed up with my wrinkle remover."

(What a Good Sport!)

- Hair dye: "Oh, goody. I'm gonna wash away those years and you won't even know me."

- A cane: "Oh, goody. Come a little closer so I can HIT YOU RIGHT IN THE MUSH, YOU INSENSITIVE, MORONIC...."

(Uh oh. Look who's being a Bad Sport.)

That's All There Is

"OK, OK, OK," someone will finally say. "Here are the *real* gifts." Oh, yeah? What a bunch of bull. Evidently you made a number of statements you would later regret. Sometime during the last year you may have mentioned that you liked the color blue or there was a robin on the front lawn or you wished you could get a little more exercise.

So now you're stuck with a sweater in a color that screams "blue light special." And some stupid exotic parakeet that begins *chirping* at 3:30 every morning. And The Amazing End-o-Lard Tummy Tucker exercise/torture device. And – from each person who doesn't really know you too well – a bouquet of one dozen helium balloons. The last time you really wanted a helium balloon was when you were eight. Thirty-two years ago. Eighty percent of your life ago. Well, now you've got at least ten dozen. Each bouquet cost more than a month's rent in your first apartment. But what the hell. At least they're not black with "R.I.P. 40" on them.

The Moral of the Story

What is the lesson to be learned here? Throughout your late 30s, don't say you like anything or indicate that you are interested in anything except money.

You may say:

- Boy, I like money.

- Gee, I could go for some money.

- Gosh, money is nice.

- Wow, I hope I get money for my birthday and not a lot of stupid presents and several hundred helium balloons.

Dream on. But, you know, those balloons would really be great if you did get that BB gun....

Chapter Three

The Physical Facts of 40

It's not as though you wake up on your 40th birthday and say, "I'm going to quit smoking and drinking, and I'm going to lose weight and get more exercise and take better care of myself." It's more like one morning, somewhere around The Big Four-O, you wake up hacking and hung over, and you can't quite get your pants buttoned without really sucking in. So you inhale deeply and, unfortunately, there's a cigarette dangling from your lips and suddenly it's half ash.

It would be very beneficial if you realized at this point that a lot of your life is half ash. But you don't.

That Little Voice

And then – maybe not that morning, but some morning just like it – the little voice in your head that has comforted you for so long stabs you right between the shoulder blades. You know the one. The one that, for all those years, has said, "So what? I don't want to live forever."

Quickly followed by:

- Make it a double.

- I don't need to jog. I have a car.

- Low-tar cigarettes are for weenies.

- Pass the bean dip.

Now the voice says, "So what? I don't want to live forever. And it's darned lucky I feel that way since I'm stuck with a bucket of sludge like you."

The Heart Attack

Perhaps you have never admitted it to anyone, but there have been times when you thought you were having a heart attack. Here's a handy way to determine whether you're really having one the next time you feel like that. Pop an antacid tablet. You know, the kind your mom or dad used to live on when you were a kid.

Don't worry. They don't taste like peppermint chalk anymore. Nowadays they taste like fruit-flavored chalk. Chew one or two or 50. If you get better, it was just heartburn. If you die, it wasn't.

Fat in Your Drain Pipe

Back in high school you never paid attention in health class when Miss Stick was talking about "Nutrition: Nature's Lincoln Logs." You were too busy trying to see whether a little cigarette smoke would come out when you forced yourself to cough deeply. Neat, huh? (Great. It's been in there since you were 15. "So what? I don't want to live forever..." Besides, all the cool kids could do it.)

The point here is that you want to know a little bit about getting healthy. Good for you. Take cholesterol, for instance. And screwed-up arteries. Your arteries are like the drain in your kitchen sink. What happens if you buy really cheap hamburger, fry it up, and dump the grease down the drain? Right. If you eat too much food that's high in cholesterol, you have several options:

- Exercise.

- Medication.

- Surgery.

- Death.

Huh? How about:

- Run hot water down the drain.

- Pour in liquid plutonium drain opener (with the fresh lemony scent!).

- Use a plumber's helper or drain snake or remove and replace the pipe.

- Move.

Oh.

What About Oat Bran?

It has been medically proven that by adding oat bran to an ordinary food item you can really jack up the price and advertise the hell out of it. Does it work? You bet! Oh, you mean health-wise.

We are not medical experts, but we do know this: The guy that played Wilbur on "Mr. Ed" is still around on stupid shows and we haven't seen Ed for a long, long time. Who ate the oats and who ate the cheeseburgers? (Obviously, this will remain a mystery until some archivist uncovers "Mr. Ed – The Lost Episodes.")

"What about Roy and Trigger?" you might ask.

Yes, Roy is still out and about and Trigger bought the farm, but then Trigger died of a broken heart, not gunked-up arteries. You see, one day Roy purchased a cheap pocket calculator and then he didn't need to drag around a hayburner to stomp on the ground and count for him.

How to Quit Smoking

If you smoke, you want to quit. Unless you're 14.

You could do it. Really. But all your Smoking Friends will hate you and hope you FAIL, FAIL, FAIL. They might still let you pal around with them, but you'll have become worse than a Non-smoking Friend. You will be an Ex-smoking Friend.

You'll talk about how you like fresh air and can taste your food and don't wheeze after strenuous exercise like stepping up on a curb. Well, they don't want to hear about it. Mostly they will hate you because, if a little twerp like you has enough willpower and determination to quit, they must really be spineless cruds.

A Happy Thought

My, this is all very depressing, isn't it? Let's talk about something pleasant: pimples. Isn't it great the way pimples have become such a fun topic now that it has been about a decade since you really had a whopper? And remember how your mom said that once you got out of your teens you wouldn't have to worry about them anymore? She was lying. She didn't really mean 20. She meant 30. Or so.

But now pimples are a great topic! As much fun as hemorrhoids used to be. Now *there's* a subject that fell right off the old chuckle chart.

Eating on the Right Side of the Bran

Speaking of which, can you believe that you've come to care about eating bran? Not lower-your-cholesterol oat bran, but plain, old-fashioned, Grandpa-used-to-eat-this-junk bran-bran. Raisin bran. Bran muffins. Bran cobbler. Bran ice cream. Bran and lobster.

Did you ever imagine there would come a time when you would have to think before you ate something?

- Is this going to keep me awake?

- Is this going to make me irregular?

- Is this going to up my cholesterol count?

- Is this going to clog my kitchen drain pipe?

- Is this going to go straight to my thighs?

That time has come. That time is now.

A Quick Quiz

"Hey," you might be saying to yourself, "I'm *not* that old and I *still* have a great sense of humor." Sure. Complete this simple statement:

Prunes are:

A. Funny.

B. Important.

See?

Stressed for Success

Stress is a very popular topic. It was discovered in the early 1980s and swept the country faster than cold pasta or flavored mineral water. No wonder you feel old!

The best way to fight stress is to buy an exercise bicycle. A lot of people find this very, very helpful. They don't have to walk all the way to the closet to hang up their clothes and they don't have to feel bad about leaving their stuff on the floor. They can just toss everything toward the bike. Then their clothes are hung up – and they can't see the bike.

In general, an exercise bike serves the same basic function as a closet doorknob but holds a lot more.

How about joining a fitness club? Now *there's* an idea. You are absolutely correct that signing a contract – What an attractive salesperson! So...healthy! – will force you to do something you don't want to do.

It will force you to make monthly payments to a club you will *never* visit.

You Are Not Alone

The experts are always saying that adolescence is a very difficult time because the young person's body is changing and he or she thinks it isn't happening to anyone else. That's true about 40, too. So let's take a load off your mind by mentioning that a lot of people your age have hair that is thinning on the tops of their heads and growing quite nicely in their nostrils.

It will get worse. Later in your life people might describe you as "bright-eyed and bushy-nosed."

You might also find it more difficult to read printed material. That doesn't mean you need reading glasses. You need longer arms.

And don't balk at the idea of bifocals. It's true you'll have to spend the first five years nodding your head as you try to adjust to far away-close up, far away-close up, far away-close up, but people around you will just assume you're a very agreeable person saying yes to everything.

Chapter Four

Sex and – Can You Believe It? – Dating

Why is it, you might be asking, that this book has to have a chapter on sex? Why is it, we reply, that you're reading this section first even though it's Chapter 4?

Grading on the Curve

You probably already know that men and women are not the same. At about age 40 a man's sex drive shifts into a lower gear

– not low gear, let's not panic here – and a woman's drive shifts into a higher gear.

This can be illustrated with a chart on which "drive" is expressed vertically and "age" is registered horizontally. Notice how "men" are curving down while "women" are perking up? See how the two paths cross, forming a giant X? Now look on the chart and check out the typical age at which the lines cross: 40. Thus, 40 is literally rated X.

Happy days are here again.

But what if your spouse is older or younger than you? In that case you have a less-than-perfect X. That's no problem. A less-than-perfect X life is better than no X life at all.

The Second Honeymoon

As you might suspect – what a lecherous mind – 40 is an ideal time for a second honeymoon. Besides providing a great atmosphere for physical closeness, it's an opportunity for you to joke about the hot time you had on your first one.

WARNING: Do this only if you are still married to the same person who was with you on your first honeymoon.

The Single Life

Maybe you're single. And sometimes you feel bad and say to yourself, "I should be married."

Just visit some friends who are wed. This is known as "keeping in touch with reality." Notice what their lives are like, how they treat each other. You'll return to your own home feeling a lot better.

The Dating Game

If you are recently divorced, well-meaning friends will urge you to go out on a date. This would be a great idea if the very thought of it did not make you want to vomit. It does.

If you are a woman, your friends know you would like to be with a fellow who is considerate, sensitive, secure, funny, caring, not bald, compassionate, and on and on and on.

If you are a man, your friends know you would like to be with a hot babe.

So, of course, the two groups match you up.

This is known as a "blind date." It means you would rather rip your eyes right out of their sockets than spend the rest of the evening with this person. But – trying to look on the bright side – even if you don't rip your eyes out, you'll never have to see this person again. She'll return to her own planet or he'll crawl back under his rock.

Classic Lines

Remember the last time you tried to get the attention of someone of the opposite sex so you could ask them on a date? You do? What a memory!

You said:

- I think we're in the same geometry class. *God*, I hate geometry.

- I've got a fake ID.

- Splash some water on your face or that tear gas will burn your eyes for hours.

- Like, I don't know, like, you know, I mean, uh, like, hi, and, you know.

You old smoothie.

The New Classics

Most likely those lines don't work anymore. Try these:

- Care to go somewhere and split a bran muffin?

- Some obscure bank in Arkansas just sent me a brand new VISA card.

- Don't think of me as a 40-year-old. Think of me as two 20s.

- "I just happen to have a copy of the doctor's report from my last checkup. Why don't you go ahead and peruse it while I take a blood sample from you for the lab?

Talk about irresistible.

And This Is My Family

Remember bringing that favorite person home to introduce to your parents? You thought nothing could be worse. Shows how stupid young people are, huh? Try bringing somebody home to introduce to your kids.

Your children can sense that this is a person you really care about, that this is serious, that this is very important to you and you are extremely vulnerable. You are dead meat.

What if you're meeting your date's kids for the first time?

DO NOT SAY:

- I know we're going to be the best of friends.

- Don't tell me your names. Let me guess who's who.

- You look just like your mom (dad).

Instead, try:

- I think your mom (dad) is too tough on you.

- I wish my kids could have come along, but they're out driving the new Porsches I just bought them.

- Here's my wallet.

Proper Attire

But it really won't matter what you say. Your date's kids won't be listening. They'll be too dumbfounded by what you're wearing. They'll sit slouched in their chairs in front of that *blaring* television set and look at you and laugh.

Laugh along. Pretend you think they're laughing at the way you say, "How do you do?" Then they'll laugh even more because you look so stupid laughing at yourself. Meanwhile they're still laughing at how you're dressed.

"Are you going to a funeral?" they'll ask.

"Oh, no," you can honestly answer. "Nothing that pleasant."

Your date will be very pleased that you and the kids are getting along so famously.

That, of course, would be the best possible outcome, so most likely it won't happen that way. Most likely the children will stare at you in sullen silence. In this case, try to charm the youngest one, that little fellow who must be in about first grade. Say: "And who's this big boy here?"

He will reply, "I gotta gun." And then his siblings will slowly smile.

You say, "What lovely teeth!" and "I'll just wait in the car."

Just for Single Parents

It should be pretty clear by now why groups for single parents are so popular. These organizations meet in public places where the children are forced to pass through metal detectors like the ones they have in airports.

These groups sponsor softball games and barbecues and swimming parties, which might seem very appealing. Why not meet some other people (chicks, guys) and at the same time let them see your kids? It certainly would save a lot of apologizing later on.

23

Consider this: Going to a single parents' group function with your kids is something like being a teenager and going to a party with your parents. Only worse. Afterall, teenagers aren't biologically to blame for their parents.

The Hot Spots

Where can you take a date when you're 40? The problem is, you still think of "dating" as something younger people do, and you have no idea what younger people are doing these days. It is very unwise to go to some place frequented by younger people. If you surround yourself with younger people, you look old.

How about dining at a nursing home cafeteria? All the residents will say, "Who are those youngsters?"

DO NOT LOOK FOR A DISCO.

That seems fairly obvious, but when the pressure is on, some people make some pretty dumb mistakes. So, no offense intended here, but:

DO NOT TRY TO DRESS, DANCE, OR TALK LIKE JOHN TRAVOLTA.

It is much better to stop by a little bistro or an espresso shop or an ethnic restaurant. Mention that you read about it in some slick magazine. Then spend the evening ripping it to shreds with cutting comments like:

- They charge so much for espresso, you'd think they'd at least give you a full-size cup, huh?

- They're supposed to have such a huge wine cellar, but did you see the way the waiter looked at me when I asked about a bottle of white infidel?

- Feel how much gum there is under here.

Dating Younger People

Who is too young for you to date? Give a potential date this simple test. Start humming a popular tune from the '50s, '60s, or '70s and then ask, "Does that sound familiar?"

If your date says, "Yes, that was a popular tune in the '50s (or '60s or '70s)," then everything is A-OK.

If he or she says, "Yeah, that's on the root beer (acne medicine, stain remover, running shoe) commercial," you should answer, "What time does your mommy want you home?"

The Best Policy

Honesty really *is* the best policy. Sooner or later, you have to be yourself. Sometimes, even after years of marriage. Start a date – a friendship, a relationship, a marriage – with the truth. Say: "I am petrified. I'm afraid I'll mess up, but I'm really glad we're going out. I was really nervous when I was getting ready. I think I put deodorant under one arm twice and forgot the other one. Just keep to my left." It shows you're human.

Be yourself. You're not as bad as you think you are. In fact, you're pretty darned good. Remember what Burt Reynolds said: "You can't hold your stomach in forever."

The Great Melting Pot

If you and that Someone Special get serious, you will have to introduce your kids to his or hers. Yes, you *have* to. Don't do it indoors.

Both sets of children will be feeling a lot of anxiety, which you can help relieve by saying to Someone Special's youngsters, "I bet my kids can beat the hell out of you. Let's find out."

The Second Marriage

If you remarry, remember that it will take time to get to know your new stepkids before you can come to love them.

Remember that you know your own kids very well and you don't even like them.

Chapter Five

Getting the Most Mileage Out of Your Mid-life Crisis

One of the best parts about turning 40 is that you are eligible to enjoy a mid-life crisis. What is mid-life? It's that period between ages 40 and 60. Give or take 10 or 20 years. What is a crisis? Being between the ages of 40 and 60. Give or take 10 or 20 years. A mid-life crisis gives you the opportunity to do something extremely stupid and not get blamed for it.

For example, you are allowed to go further into debt by buying a wonderful red Alfa Romeo. Or you can purchase a four-wheel-drive pickup truck. Or quit your job at the bank to make copper wire jewelry. Or quit making copper wire jewelry and get a job at a bank.

You may do just about anything, as long as it makes very little sense and your friends and family think you have gone nuts.

The Catch

The problem is, you may do only *one* thing. Do not squander your crisis on the first stupid idea that pops into your head when you wake up on your 40th birthday. Do not skip work that day. Or go fly a kite. Or have pizza delivered for breakfast.

Social scientists – geeks who are given large federal grants to call people up and ask them questions that would land the rest of us in jail ("Are you wearing any shoes? Are you wearing stockings? Have you painted your toes?") – social scientists have discovered that women tend to hold on to their opportunity to fall apart while men use it right away.

Think of the MLC (mid-life crisis) as a Get-Out-of-Jail-Free card in Monopoly. Sometimes it's better to pay the $50 or spend three turns in the pokey or take a chance on getting doubles rather than slap that card down on the table.

For Men Only

Some men also suffer from the ego-shattering embarrassment of Premature Male Mid-life Crisis (also known as Male Mental Pause). Here's this poor fellow, still in his 30s, and suddenly he quits his job and announces to the world that he's going to try out for the Lakers, or move to Tahiti and take up painting turtles and sand dollars for a living.

Everyone around him smiles and nods and thinks, "That's it, babe. That was your one shot."

If you are a gent who is still in his 30s and you have been tempted to go ahead and have your MLC, we HIGHLY recommend that instead you:

- Grow your beard. Shave your beard. Grow your beard. Shave your beard. Grow....

- Buy a chain saw. Even one of those wimpy electric ones with less power than a cheap sewing machine will do. The saw doesn't matter as much as the gloves you buy to go with it. Leather. Yellow. Expensive. You don't have to saw anything. Just wear the gloves. Sniff them when you feel the urge to announce you're heading to Alaska to pan for gold.

- Become an expert on something. Anything. The inner workings of nuclear energy. The path to world peace. How to transfer a call on your office's new phone system.

The Old Album

This would be a good time to dust off the old family album and look at some of the people from your past. See all those old, tired, wrinkled relatives? They were in their 30s.

And, as long as we're on the subject, remember those two old ladies who lived down the block when you were a kid? Late 20s.

And old man Foster, the duffer who did odd jobs around your place? Nineteen.

And that wicked babysitter who scared the living graham crackers out of you? Eleven. But she was very, very tall.

The Inventor

Carl Jung was a Swiss psychiatrist who invented the mid-life crisis. He was a real Freud fan until he hit his mid-30s, and then he went out in his backyard and made mud pies for a while and came up with a whole new theory about that web of psychosis known as your personality. This is the truth. Pretty darned weird, huh?

Jung (pronounced "young," as in "The Jung and the Restless") said that you spend the first half of your life trying to please others and the second half saying, "Forget that noise." He used bigger words to say it. His theory was confirmed by Ricky Nelson, who sang a song about a garden party and how he'd drive a truck before he'd keep performing those stupid songs he sang on "Ozzie and Harriet."

Why does this mid-life change occur? Maybe because life offers lessons that are hard to ignore. The main one is: People you love die and they don't get to take all their junk with them when they go.

Maybe there is more to living than accumulating stuff.

The Group

Maybe you should join a group. A group is made up of a bunch of people who are pretty much the same and who get together and chew the fat until they discover they are a bunch of people who are pretty much the same. A group is never as interesting or entertaining as the people who met with Dr. Bob Hartley once a week in downtown Chicago. (By the way, we don't want to throw mud on the entire psychological profession, but after dropping out of sight for a short while, Dr. Bob turned up at a Vermont inn with a different name and a different wife and, as if that's not bad enough, he claims to make a living writing how-to books. Whew! Talk about your sickos.)

So, should you join a group? If you're not sure, you might consider joining a group of people who are considering joining a group.

Maybe you need a little one-on-one counseling. You don't? Why do you say that? Why do you ask, "What does that question mean?" What does that question mean to you? Do you think it's supposed to mean something?

Back to School

You could go back to school. Of course, that can get confusing because there are several different kinds of institutions of higher learning. Here's a list to help you make the right choice:

- University: Here you have to spend a lot of money, take a lot of classes that have nothing to do with what you want to learn, and be surrounded by students who are younger than some of your sweaters.

- Special College for Middle-Aged People Who Don't Want to Go to a University: These places cater to mid-life crisis people such as yourself, but they never have a good football team and you have to spend a lot of time arguing with your family and friends that "It is SO a real college!"

- National Institute of (fill in the blank): These are the places that advertise on the local TV station all day long while you watch "The Rockford Files" or "Perry Mason" or "The Love Connection." They will help you learn all about driving semis or making it in The World of Fashion or becoming a prison guard. (Some people are so taken in by these ads that they attend all the institutes and become the envy of their friends because they enjoy the very financially and personally rewarding profession of Security Officer at a Truck Stop Boutique.)

An Easier Way

It is much, much easier to simply get a job with a different company or in a different field by using a tried and true method: lie.

This is done with a resume. A fancy-shmancy French word for "horse manure."

Give it a try. Which sounds better to you?

1. "I really want this job. Here's my resume."

2. "I really want this job. Here's my horse manure."

But keep in mind that no interviewer or boss-to-be ever actually reads your resume. What are you, crazy? He or she received several *hundred thousand* of them after putting that little ad in Sunday's classified section.

What the boss does is choose the five or six that are on the nicest paper and look the neatest. Some books, like the best-seller, *How to Get That Job For Which You Are Totally Unqualified*, suggest using bright paper for your resume. That's pretty risky. Yes, a hot pink sheet will stand out, but would you really want to work for a person attracted to hot pink?

Avoiding Stress

Do yourself – and your poor, aging heart – a favor.

- Do *not* type up your resume on company time with a company typewriter or word processor.

- Do *not* use the company photocopy machine to run off duplicates of your resume.

Your boss will pop out of the woodwork and say, "What's that you're working on?" and the copy machine will jam with your resume stuck in its gut. Instead, break into the office at night to do your typing and rent a U-Haul trailer to steal the copy machine.

Proper Attire

Let's say you get called in for an interview. (Oh, come on, we're trying to be upbeat here! Especially since your life is half over and you haven't accomplished squat.) You want to be sure to dress nicely. The problem is, if you dress nicely, people at the place where you currently work will say, "Ha ha! What's with you? Got a job interview or something?"

You say:

1. I'm going to my mother's funeral. Are we still on for bowling tonight?

2. These were the only clean clothes I could find this morning.

3. I always wear a tux (gown).

We recommend the funeral line. That gives you a good excuse for missing two hours of work. It's also much less painful than claiming you had to go to the dentist and then ripping out a tooth with vise-clamp pliers to back up your story.

The Interview

As you're sitting in that little reception area, waiting for your interview, you might think this is the worst thing that could possibly happen to you. You might think you could not be more nervous. Sure you could. You could be waiting to go out on a date.

Feel better now? Here's some advice:

- Think positive!

- Act professional!

- Lie your brains out.

Remember that the moment always comes when the interviewer asks, "Do you have any questions?" If you say "no," does that mean you get along well with people and won't make any waves, or does it mean you are really stupid because anyone with even half a brain would have a whole truckload of questions? For example: "Do I get the job?" "When do I get a raise?" "You don't expect me to put in overtime, do you?" and "How much do *you* get paid?"

The solution is to ask a question not directly related to the interview or the job. Say: "Is that a poppy seed or a little bug between your teeth?"

We're kidding! DON'T SAY THAT! That was a joke. Nobody is going to hire you if you talk about "little bugs." Say: "Is that a poppy seed or a small insect between your teeth?"

You're hired.

Chapter Six

The Middle Generation

At about this time in your life, you are the "middle generation." This means you have both parents and children to tell you what a horrible person you are and to make you feel guilty.

Basic Statesmanship

Your folks and your kids are probably very good buddies. This alliance is based on a solid principle: The enemy of my enemy is my friend.

It is a major mistake to let them spend much time together. All they have in common is you and your stupidity. Your parents can tell your kids how dumb you were 35 or more years ago and your kids can tell your parents how dumb you were this morning. It's too bad they both fail to notice that at least you're consistent. That ought to count for something.

Being Cool

Some 40-year-olds try to recapture their youth by attempting to be friends with their children. They try to dress cool. Look cool. Talk cool.

But that's not possible. You and your children live in different worlds. (Fall down on your knees and thank almighty God for that.) Your kids don't try to be "cool." They try to be "way cool" or "mass cool" or "way mass cool." Or at least they did a week or two ago. Today...who knows?

Whatever you say or do, *it will be wrong.* Remember when you were young and you got all set to go out, and you thought you looked groovy and your mom said you looked like the bee's knees?

It's Called Fashion

One of the hardest things for you to get used to is your son or daughter spending a bundle – your money, of course – on an item of clothing very similar to one you tossed into a Salvation Army bin 20 years ago. That old baseball jacket. Those cheap canvas sneakers. The high-top basketball shoes.

Here's a little tip: If one of your kids looks like he's all dressed up for a '50s or '60s costume party with rolled up blue jeans, slicked-back hair, basic T-shirt, and high tops, *don't say anything.*

And don't scream. You are not really trapped in a time warp. (But wouldn't this have made a dandy "Twilight Zone?")

Once again, we urge you to look on the bright side. You know *exactly* where to search him to find that pack of cigarettes.

Truly Filthy

As long as we're on the subject of tobacco, here's a good example of your child taking a disgusting habit and putting a particularly revolting twist on it: chewing tobacco. More accurately called "spitting" or "drooling" tobacco.

Now the last time chewing tobacco looked even vaguely amusing to you was when the old guy in *Butch Cassidy and the Sundance Kid* – the guy going up and down the mountain in Bolivia – would spit and then curse and wipe off his chin with his shirt sleeve. And then he got shot. Very dead. Before that the same guy was the head of the prison in *Cool Hand Luke*, the gentleman who worried about people who failed to communicate. There is a moral here. If you mess with Paul Newman in one movie, he will make you spit on yourself and get shot in the next. Fair is fair.

What does this have to do with your child and turning 40? Well...nothing. But it's pretty darned interesting and it did take your mind off that wad in your kid's mouth.

When It Was Your Turn

Don't forget that your generation put a spin on the old tobacco issue, too. Remember when your dad caught you that evening?

"You roll your own cigarettes?" he asked.

"Yeah," you answered. "Are the Oreos all gone?"

No way! You didn't say that! Who are you kidding? Trying to make yourself sound so hip. You said:

"No, Dad. It's incense. Are the Oreos all gone?"

What About Dear Old Dad?

Your dad had the same problem. Well, not exactly the same. Someone walked in on him when he was puffing away on a cigarette and said, "What the hell are you doing, boy?"

And your old man – Mr. Iceblock – said, "Uhhhhhhh...."

"No son of mine is going to smoke cigarettes!"

"Uhhh...."

"Those are for people with loose morals. Here. Take one of my cigars."

"Thank you, Mama."

Raising Your Parents

One of your biggest problems is that you are now assuming so much of the responsibility that once belonged to your grandmother – that sweet, little, cigar-chewing lady. You have become your parents' parent. Yes, you have. You *have*! Do these sound familiar?

- Be sure to keep your front door locked.

- It isn't safe to be out after dark.

- You look tired. Would you like to take a nap?

- Are you eating right?

- You haven't forgotten to take your medication, have you?

- Let's not watch this movie. It's rated R. How about seeing *Lady and the Tramp* one more time?

- You're just being stubborn. I know what's best for you even if you don't. GO TO YOUR ROOM!

That's about all you ever say to your parents anymore.

License to Terrorize

Speaking of touchy subjects, here's one you've been avoiding for quite some time: How are you going to get your parents off the road?

You just couldn't believe it when the state renewed their driver's licenses. It was pretty obvious there was no driving test. Or written test. Or eye test. The state says they drive just fine. The insurance company gives them a discount because people their age are such good drivers. HA!

You know how your mom always fiddles with the rearview mirror. You know how your dad always gets distracted trying to scrape that blob of dried egg yolk off his shirt. ("EGGS! Dad, what have I told you about cholesterol?") You know they are horrible drivers!

But, hey, don't be picking on senior citizens. Don't stereotype them. It so happens your folks were always horrible drivers. They taught you, didn't they?

98.6° Fahrenheit

There is one thing you've noticed about your parents and your friends' parents, but nobody ever seems to talk about it. Their thermostat is busted.

Somewhere along the way they decided they really, really, really like to live in a home that is hot enough to wilt orchids. Even in the dead of winter you have to wear a sleeveless shirt and shorts when you stop in to see your mom or dad. You know it's going to be well over 100 degrees in there. Well over. You could bake cookies right on the kitchen counter. ("No, Mom, don't turn on the oven!")

What's wrong with them? Nothing. Except they don't know how to tell you that they don't want another stupid sweater for their birthday, Christmas, Hanukkah, Mother's Day, Father's Day, or any other stupid day! Before you show up they say, "Oh, our darling child is coming by! Let's crank the furnace up to 130 degrees and hope our offspring comes to realize that we have heat in this place and we don't want another stinking cardigan!"

They love you dearly. Even if sometimes you are so very slow.

I Said, "CAN YOU TURN DOWN...?"

That kind of makes you wonder about other things, too, doesn't it? The television set, for example. How come it's always on and very loud when you stop by? The truth is, their hearing is fine and they don't really even like that particular program.

They just don't want to talk to you because you are very, very boring.

Into the Closet

As a matter of fact, they'd send you to your old bedroom if they hadn't converted it into a closet.

See? There you go again. It isn't really a closet. Now they call it the "guest room." All they did was sell your old bed, fill the room with boxes, and put up shelves and coat hanger racks. But it's *not* a closet. Geez, you're touchy.

So stop whining about the guest room. And nobody wants to hear how – on the day you moved out – your parents changed all the outside locks. Cut them some slack! They thought it would be rude to ask you to give back your key.

The Outlaw

In an earlier chapter we mentioned how much fun it is to marry someone who already has a carload of kids. Well, right up there on the same I-Think-I'm-Getting-A-Migraine scale are your in-laws.

Yes, spending time with them really helps you understand why your spouse is so...so...so.... Yes, it helps, but at what price? Even figuring out how to enter their home is a challenge. If you go first, ahead of your spouse, you knock and wait to be admitted. But if your spouse is ahead of you, he or she just walks right in and says, "I thought I told you the front door should be kept locked. God, it's hot in here. What are you watching. WHAT ARE YOU WATCHING?"

You've Got Their Number

At least now when you visit your in-laws they no longer say to your spouse, "Hello, honey. Who's that with you?" No, they don't do that anymore. But they sure as hell never seem to recognize your voice on the phone.

So when you do telephone, you need to say, "Hello, Mother/Dad (their last name). This is (your name). I married your son/daughter, (spouse's name). I'm calling to... to...."

Of course, by then you've forgotten why you called and your parent-in-law says, "Who *is* this? What kind of jerk would call up and then not even... oh. It's you."

See? They're getting to know you. Things are a lot better than you think.

Less Than Perfect

At this point in your life, it finally dawns on you that really and truly your parents are not perfect. Never were and never will be. And your children are not perfect. Never were and never will be. And you are not perfect. Never were but maybe someday.... No. Never will be.

And for some absolutely unknown and unfathomable reason, you really love your parents. And your kids. And it seems like the time is right to forgive them for the bad things and thank them for the good. You realize they love you. Little, old imperfect you. In their unique way, they love you.

Chapter Seven

The Middle Manager

You've been out in the work force for a while now and have probably settled into that very comfortable spot known as "middle management."

You have bosses yelling at you, "Make those peons work faster!" And workers yelling at you, "Tell those slave drivers to drop dead!" No matter who's mad at whom, you manage to be right in the middle of it.

At least you're needed.

The Dinosaurs

Remember when you first started working? It was so much fun to get together with other workers about the same age and talk about the dinosaurs that roamed the halls.

You know, the ones who had to have it done a certain way. Who had a fit if you happened to be a minute or two late in the morning. Who yapped and yapped and yapped at staff meetings but never said anything. Who dressed like Aunt Bea or Barney Fife.

You and your friends used to hang out in the company lunchroom during breaks, and then one of the dinosaurs would come lumbering in and all of you would stop talking. Then the dinosaur would get a cup of prune juice or something and lumber out and all of you would burst out laughing.

Sometimes, when you felt a little guilty, you wondered if the dinosaur could hear that laughing from the hallway. Now you know. You, Big Four-O Birthday Person, are a dinosaur.

"No way!" you say.

Oh, yeah?

Haven't you noticed how all the old dinosaurs keep retiring? You used to think, "Good, pretty soon there will only be young people around here." Now you think, "God, pretty soon there will only be young people around here." Still don't believe it?

Which are you?

Person A: "Ten years ago we tried doing it that way and it didn't work."

Person B: "Ten years ago I was in the eighth grade."

Suddenly your sense of time is all shot to smithereens. You'd be fine if you didn't have to work with all these youngsters who say they're adults.

Here's another tip: If you didn't like the snotty remark from person B, that former eighth-grader, don't say anything about your favorite coffee mug. You've been using it since she was seven.

Peace, Man!

It's the little things that will trip you up. Remember how you used to wait until one of the dinosaurs said something really stupid and then you would run to the normal people (people in their early 20s) and repeat it?

Well...the other day you made the mistake of mentioning Woodstock.

And the kid answered, "I didn't know somebody your age would still read the funnies. Is *Peanuts* your favorite?"

And you said, "New York!"

And she said, "I guess I'm not familiar with that one. I'm sure it's very amusing. Does it have larger type or something?"

And you said, "Half a million!"

And the kid said, "Uh huh, fine, good, don't excite yourself," and went tearing down the hall toward the lunchroom.

Maybe things would be all right if you could just stay away from these tykes, but you can't, because one of them is your boss. How did that happen?

Who knows? The mucky-mucks must have had a conference and said, "We don't want somebody with experience and talent and a proven track record, we want some kid who will spend a good one-fourth of his gross income on hair-styling mousse."

It's pretty obvious they said something like that, anyway.

Error

Your mistake was walking around saying, "We should provide a quality product or service at a reasonable price and back that up with an ironclad guarantee." You chump! You sound like you actually *believe* the commercials your company puts out. The only reason you got to be a middle manager was because all the other workers were complaining about how you wanted to be on the no-managers-allowed company softball team and nobody knew how to tell you politely to take a hike.

But for a *real* boss, the mucky-mucks wanted a go-getter who would gladly rip out a fellow worker's heart with her bare hands if it meant advancing her career. Or even get her a better parking space.

And then there's you. You still bring in homemade cookies for people's birthdays.

Junior Executive

But give The Baby Boss a chance. Even when you meet him on that first day and he's chewing grape bubble gum. Don't say, "I hope you brought enough for the rest of the office, young man."

All those years of keeping a straight face around the dinosaurs was good practice for The Baby Boss. Now you can just nod and look fascinated when he says, "You know what! I just found out we're on something called a 'fiscal year.' I'm not sure what that is, but I think it means we get two New Year's Eve parties!"

What You Did Wrong

Getting worker bees to do what the queen bee wants is a piece of cake compared to trying to train The Baby Boss. So, of course, training The Baby Boss is part of your job. The mucky-mucks have great faith in you. You know exactly what needs to be done in that position. "Then why," you might be tempted to ask, "didn't they promote me?"

You applied. You bought a new suit. They interviewed you. Everything seemed to be going swell until a member of the panel said, "You are a part of that pain-in-the-butt generation that cost all of us old people a lot of time and money. Now it's our turn to get even. You're about the same age as a child of mine and since I can no longer punish him, I'll have to settle for punishing you. We're going to hire somebody from the *next* generation. Somebody who is greedy and amoral just like we are! Somebody who will make your last 25 years with this company a living hell."

What? You didn't hear him say that? Well, you have to read between the lines. His exact words were, "Thank you. We'll let you know what our decision is."

Your Special Day

And now it's your birthday. Take comfort in the fact that not all your co-workers will make a big deal out of your turning 40. In fact, quite a few of them will say, "Oh, yeah? I thought you were older than that."

There's no point in trying to hide your age. The old grapevine has already broadcast "The Big Four-O." It's a hot topic. And it will be, all day long. If you're not careful, it might be the lead story. The best way to avoid this situation is to start a more interesting rumor first thing in the morning. Something like:

- Guess which receptionist is pregnant?

- Guess which boss's son was arrested last night for possession of a controlled substance?

- Guess which receptionist is pregnant by which boss's son who got arrested last night for possession of a controlled substance?

You probably won't get a gift or a card, but maybe some people will take up a collection. You can always use another 43 cents. Or maybe some people will sign the back of an old memo.

Or maybe, too bad for you, you'll have to share the day with everyone there who has a birthday that month. In your case, it will probably be – you guessed it – The Baby Boss.

He will be real chummy and say, "Forty! My mom is in her 40s!"

You answer, "Oh, yeah? Didn't she used to be a receptionist who went out with a boss's son who was arrested for possession of a controlled substance?"

Some co-workers might take you out for a fancy lunch. Live it up. Order the large fries. Get a little apple pie, too. Don't forget that "take you out for lunch" is not the same as "take you out and buy you lunch."

The High School Class Reunion

The invitation is sitting on the dresser in your bedroom, isn't it? You don't know how they got your new address, but you do know there's *no way* you're going to the 20th anniversary reunion of your high school graduation.

Not you. Uh uh. No way. Case closed. Absolutely, positively....

Don't forget to pack your old yearbook.

Wait a minute. Most kids are 17 or 18 when they graduate from high school. Boy, you sure wouldn't have described yourself as a "kid" when you were 17 or 18, would you? You thought you were all grown up and knew the answer to everything, and you didn't mind sharing it. Especially with somebody old. Somebody 19.

Anyway, your class should have had its 20th reunion two years ago. So how come they're having one now? Mainly because your class still can't get it together on time. Couldn't then, can't now.

Commencing

And, as a matter of fact, your class wasn't the brightest in the world. Remember the three covaledictorians? It took that many to get final grades that added up to a B-plus. Remember the commencement ceremonies? Your principal, Mr. Balding, said, "Now the covaledictorians will speak...

Roll over...

And play dead."

On the List

How the heck did the reunion committee get you on its list anyway? Especially after you moved so many times. Got married and divorced and changed your name a few times. Went into hiding after all those hounding letters from the Book of the Month Club. Doggone it. Maybe you *should* have had that sex-change operation. Too late now.

This was your mistake: You ran into an old classmate (all your classmates are old) at the supermarket and you said, "Is that you? Ha ha ha! You're fat and bald and look like hell!" She didn't appreciate your attitude. She found out where you're living and zipped off a note to your old school. She turned you in.

Once again, you're too late. But this is what you should have said when you ran into that classmate:

- Excuse me, stranger.

- Is that you? Or are you your younger and very handsome sibling who was just a kid when us old-timers were in high school?

- I won't turn you in if you don't turn me in.

- I'm not going to any stupid reunion. Are you going to the stupid reunion? I don't know anybody who's going to the stupid reunion.

So who's going to the stupid reunion, besides you?

- People who have made a lot of money.

- People who are famous. (The guy who does traffic reports on the radio, for example.)

- People who have grown taller.

- People who have lost weight.

- People who have gained weight and then lost weight.

- People with a lot of hair, none of which is gray.

- People whose lives crumbled after high school and who want to come back and relive those glory days, the happiest days of their pathetic little lives.

- People who don't want their former classmates to think there's something wrong with them.

The Organizers

Just who is putting this whole thing together, anyway?

Every reunion committee includes:

1. A former cheerleader.

2. A former student body president or class officer.

3. A former sucker who volunteered for every cruddy job that came down the pike and lived for pep rallies.

4. A geek who wants to show everyone in the in-crowd that he doesn't even think about the in-crowd anymore and to prove it to the in-crowd he's going to help organize a reunion where he can mingle with the in-crowd.

Guess what the reunion committee members are up to these days:

1. The former cheerleader now sells cosmetics or kitchen plasticware or voodoo vitamins.

2. The former class president now sells insurance or real estate or all-purpose home cleaning products.

3. The former sucker is now the development director for your old high school.

4. The former geek is still a geek.

The True You

These organizers are the ones who sent you the letter and the form entitled, "All About Me." You were supposed to fill it out and send it back. *Right away!*

Send your resume. No point in coming up with a new set of lies. If you don't have one, borrow one from a neighbor or co-worker who is successful. But don't bother sending a current photo.

The Schedule

You'll notice on the reunion schedule that a lot of the activities are only tentatively planned. You might not really take the Concord to Paris. You might have a sock hop in the gym instead. In general, no matter what propaganda you receive, the reunion weekend will go something like this:

Friday evening: Arrive at moderately priced hotel, meet in medium-sized ballroom, get drunk quickly.

Saturday morning: Vomit, take aspirin, and order juice from room service.

Saturday noon: Informal brunch ($15 for coffee, a small juice, and one dry sweet-roll).

Saturday afternoon: Festive bus tour to some god-awful place your parents used to drag you to, kicking and screaming.

Saturday night: Big-deal banquet and dance.

Sunday morning: See Saturday morning.

Sunday afternoon: Cry all the way home.

"That's really what it's going to be like?" you ask. Don't you wish. You should be so lucky.

Travel Light

The problems begin before you even get there. For example: Do you take your spouse with you?

No, because he or she always embarrasses you.

Yes, because you don't want your old classmates to think you married someone who always embarrasses you.

What you should do is.... Oh, come now. Aren't you a little old to just be *given* the answers? Aren't there some things you can decide for yourself?

The question is, do you force your spouse to come along, doubling the cost, and then listen to him or her gripe all the time about what a stupid class you have and what a stupid school it must have been and what a stupid idea it was to come to this stupid reunion? Or do you drop him or her like a hot rock and go alone?

Here's a hint: Thud.

A Bright Spot

The reunion doesn't have to be totally bleak. Try to find that kid who flunked fifth grade, the kid who shaved twice a day when he was 16 and bought you and your buddies beer because he looked so old. Just imagine what he looks like now!

Stand next to him for any photos. You'll look young.

On the Make

You'll notice some very nice-looking people at the reunion. Like that sweet young thing over there. She doesn't seem to be dragging a spouse around. Why not stop over and say, in a very deep and sexy voice, "Hello"?

This is why not:

She will answer, "Well, hello," and then she'll glance at your name tag. "I remember you," she'll say. She does! "You still owe me a book report. I should never have let you pass senior English."

Miss Stratford! Perfect. You just tried to pick up one of your old teachers. "Old"? She was 22 when you were a senior. It was her first year of teaching. Now she's 44 and you're 40 and she's a fox and you're going to have to spend the rest of the weekend reading the Cliffs Notes on 1984, the book about society far in the future.

No, you're not going to have to do that. Come on. You're all grown up now. Just say, "I left it on your desk."

Your Mentor

Hey, maybe some other teachers will be there. Maybe that favorite one of yours. The one who inspired you to...to...to....

Well, so you feel you haven't really accomplished anything. He was a decent guy anyway, and you'd like to thank him for being a good teacher. A rare bird. And there he is! (You can't figure out why all these teachers are here. What you don't know is that faculty members get free eats and booze at all school reunions.)

So you walk up and say, "I want to thank you, sir, for being one of the best teachers I ever had. No. The best. Number one."

And he'll answer, "Who are you?"

Give him a break. He's old. He's 50. Introduce yourself.

Then he'll say, "Oh, yes, I remember your younger sister. Brilliant. A delight. One of my best students. How is she doing?"

One Pair, Two Pair, Three of a Kind

Sometime during the weekend you will find yourself in the middle of a serious game of Alumni Poker. In this game you try to impress people by lying about how successful you are.

"I make $150,000 a year."

"I weigh three pounds less than I did my senior year."

"I have a condo in Aspen."

"I just bought a new Mercedes."

And on and on and on.

Until, if you're lucky, somebody has the courage to say, "I don't make much money, but I really like what I'm doing."

Or: "I don't go out on the town much anymore. I'd rather spend a quiet evening with one or two good friends."

Or: "I haven't had any stress headaches since I turned down a promotion that would have meant moving to another part of the country."

Or: "I have a really nice family. I love my wife and kids."

Look around at these people. They were a mixed group in high school. Some were almost all grown up physically and others still pretty much looked and talked like kids. Now some are grown up in a different way and others only want to talk about cars and condos and corporate salaries.

Just like kids.

Chapter Nine

You Can't Go Home Again – But Then Why Would You Want To?

You're pretty typical if you feel a deep-seated urge to return to your old hometown and see the house you lived in when you were a kid. But don't plan on taking your spouse and kids with you.

A Moving Experience

Do you know how many times the average 40-year-old has moved during his or her lifetime? Somewhere right around… a lot.

You probably grew up in another state and didn't care when you left it because you thought, "I'm getting out of this one-horse, nowhere place." And now you want to return. That should give you a pretty good indication of how your life has progressed. "Nowhere" has become a step up. A dream vacation.

After listening to you yap all these years about your old home-town and how great it was, your spouse and kids will want to go with you when you head back to see it, even though the words they use don't really convey the excitement they feel. They will say, "Do we hafta?" and, "Gross."

Faded Photographs

The first thing you will notice about your old hometown is that it is no longer your old hometown, which exists now only in some very cruddy photographs in an old Buster Brown shoebox some-where. A bunch of snapshots your mom has been meaning to put in the family album since Lyndon Johnson was… *Vice President*.

Let's say your town has prospered. This means your home – your roots, the core of your existence – is now one of the following:

1. A parking lot.

2. A Taco Bell.

3. A Taco Bell parking lot.

Your old bedroom is back by the cheese grater.

Just about now your kids are going to start asking questions. Things like:

- Is this where you grew up?

- Why does your old neighborhood smell like refried beans?

- Did your mom let you skateboard in this parking lot?

- Can you roll down your window? I think I'm getting carsick again.

Don't get alarmed. Not every 40-year-old's former home has been torn down and replaced by a fast-food Mexican restaurant. Some have been torn down and replaced by a national donut chain or a bargin shoe store.

If your town has pretty much died or your neighborhood has become what is generally known as a lower-socioeconomic area, speed by your old homestead but do not stop. Point it out to your children as you blitz by it and be sure to mention that when you lived there it wasn't a crack house.

A Matter of Perception

If, by some miracle, your old home is still standing and isn't being used as a house of ill repute, take a stroll around. Notice how the "big back yard" has shrunk. How the "little tree" has grown. How the current occupants are calling the cops because some weirdo is walking around their yard taking pictures.

Why not knock on the front door and introduce yourself? Say: "Hi! I'm me and I used to live here a long time ago. Would you mind if I looked around inside?"

- "Would you mind if I took a photo or two?"

- "Would you mind pointing that gun somewhere else?"

Then, as you stand on your old front porch while the current occupants try to keep a tight grip on the collars of their pit bulls, you can also ask, "Do the Joneses still live down the block? Or the Smiths? Or the Ogrodowskis?"

And the current occupants will reply, "Thank God. There's the patrol car now."

Officer Friendly

What do you say to this burly police officer who is popping the snap on his holster as he walks your way? You say, "Aren't you little Timmy?" Sure enough! It's your old best friend's baby brother. All grown up. And up. And up.

This is *great*! You can talk about old times. How you and your friend used to ditch him and take his candy and laugh at him when he wet his pants.

Then again, maybe this isn't a good time to reminisce. But it is a very good time to say, "Hello, Tim. I hope you don't remember me and I hope you take bribes. Are traveler's checks OK?"

Also on the Tour

Now it's time to show your family the rest of the old hometown.

Take them to the library and to the church or synagogue and tell them how much time you used to spend there.

Be sure to check a map beforehand so you can find these places. Better still, just point anywhere and say, "That was where my family used to worship every week. There, where that frozen yogurt shop is." And, "Oh, hell, they tore down the library."

Don't mention that your home away from home was that sleazy tavern on the outskirts of town, the one that charged double for watered-down drinks but never asked to see an I.D. The one you spent most of high school in.

While we're on the subject, can you even *remember* the last time you got "carded" – to prove you were 21? You can?

Guess that shows how memorable – and infrequent – an event it is. And speaking of memory, we want to tell you once again that you don't need to worry just because yours is slipping. Yes, we've said this in every chapter so far but, sad to say, some 40-year-olds won't recall it. Thank goodness you're not one of those. But keep that I.D. handy. It won't be too long before you'll need it to prove to merchants that you don't deserve the senior citizen discount.

A Teachable Moment

After surviving for four decades, you've learned a thing or two from all that you've experienced. This trip back home gives you a wonderful opportunity to teach these things to your kids. You picked up a lot of wisdom in this old hometown and, because you're such a peach, you feel obligated to share some of it with your young ones.

Go ahead. As you drive along, say, "I'd like to share with you some of the most important things I learned in this town. Some things that might make your lives a little easier. The main one is this: When you grow up, don't *ever* take your spouse and children back to your hometown.

Look at the expressions on their faces! It's like... like... you finally got through to them! Listen to what they have to share with you: "There's a McDonald's!"

Chapter Ten

Bluff Your Way Through the Classics

Now that you're getting on in years, you might take stock of your life and say, "There are so many things I haven't learned. There must be some way to fake it."

Good news. There is.

A Classical Education

For you, a "classic" is a tune by the Righteous Brothers or the "old" Coke from a bottle. That is *not* what we mean here. We mean that really highbrow stuff that makes you sound snotty as hell.

You know.

- Architecture.

- Poetry.

- Ballet.

- Opera.

- Etiquette.

- French wine.

- Who most recently slept with whom on "All My Children."

We're sure you already have some of this down.

You want to become cultured, or what is commonly known as a Renaissance man or woman. If you study this chapter carefully, you'll be so highbrow your friends and family won't even recognize you.

Now *there's* a goal everyone wants to shoot for.

The Pesky Preposition

Oh, my! Did you notice how that last sentence ended? It's not unusual for a child to do something like that, but an adult could be in serious trouble for letting his preposition hang out in public. Do not end a sentence with a preposition. (You might be asking, "What is a preposition?" A preposition is a little word with which you're not supposed to end a sentence.)

In the previous section, for example, it would have been much better to say, "Now there's a goal everyone wants to shoot for, huh?" Make a note of it.

A Danger

The problem with being hoity-toity about grammar, however, is that there is always someone hoity-toitier than you just ready to jump down your throat.

Some people are famous for their use of correct grammar. Edwin Newman, for one. No, he is not the bucktoothed, big-eared guy in *Mad* magazine. That's his brother, Alfred E., who never learned to talk good and always misspells his last name.

Edwin is the one who says, "What...I worry?"

Basic Guidelines

There are entire books written on correct grammar. Don't let them fool you. They're short, but they don't have any pictures. So the only rules you have to follow are:

1. If it sounds wrong, it's right. ("I'm going to make a wonderful Renaissance man, am I not?")

2. When in doubt, throw it out. ("Marie, please lay/lie the book on the table." No, no, no. "Marie, howsabout you chuck the book over on that there table?")

Yes, But What Is...?

What is the "Renaissance"? (Literally, "naissance again.") It's obvious you need a little help with history. Let's begin with the well-known admonition, "Those who do not know their history are doomed to hear a stupid quote about history written by some guy who is probably dead by now."

"History" is all about a bunch of white guys in Europe who went all over the world stealing property from guys who weren't white, and in some places the thieves' descendants still have it.

This, of course, is the classical definition and that's what we're after here. The quintessential example – Hey, we're really trying to get you into the spirit of this chapter – the quintessential example is Christopher Columbus. He sailed west and hit something and said, "I've discovered land!" And the people who had been living there for thousands of years looked down and said, "Is that what this is!"

Did you ever notice how the history books pretty much gloss over the fact that C.C. had no idea where he was? He thought he was in Indiana. And now you know the rest of the story.

The Only Term You Need to Know

Let's move on to architecture because this is a very easy subject. You do not need to know the difference between a dork column and an idiotic column. You do need to be familiar with the term "flying buttress." Flying buttresses are what hold up Notre Dame's walls. That's in Paris, France, not South Bend, Indiana. That Columbus story really threw you for a loop, didn't it? Christopher Columbus, not Columbus, Ohio. No problem with geography here.

Anyway, you need to be familiar with the term "flying buttress," because you never know when you'll find yourself in France looking at an old cathedral or out on your front lawn looking at your neighbor in her new shorts.

Proper Etiquette

Not that you would mention it to her. No, no. That would be a breach of etiquette. (You would mention it to your neighbor on the other side and watch as the news circled the block and got back to the cathedral in question.)

Just like grammar, there are basic rules that cover most questions of etiquette.

Rule 1: Follow the example set by the hostess.

Now that shouldn't be too tough unless, of course, you don't know what a hostess is. Try this simple test:

- A hostess is:
  A. The woman to whose home I have been invited.
  B. Twinkies, cupcakes, and – whatchamacallits, those ones with coconut – Sno Balls.

Well, it's pretty obvious that....

Ding Dongs, Ho Hos, fruit pies – although the good ones aren't really fruit but are filled with lemon or chocolate pudding...

Fine. Just one more point about etiquette and we'll move on.

Rule 2: Start from the outside.

Say you're at a very fancy dinner party and there are two or three dozen gleaming pieces of silverware surrounding your plate. The first course is served. You wonder what it is. You say, "Do you mind if I eat this outside?"

Foreign Languages

You probably don't remember much from that year or two of foreign language class you had to take in high school. What was it, English?

In any case, don't bother signing up now for any language course called, "For the Traveler." Who needs to spend all that money and six long weeks learning how to say: "Excuse me, is this what people in your country really use for toilet paper?"

Instead, just stay right here in this country and say to people, "Well, you know what the (fill in the blank) say!" French, Germans, Italians, Japanese.... Everyone will assume there is some very pithy....

(Say! Have you noticed how we're tossing in some terrific words in this chapter? Straight from *Thirty Days to a Gooder Vocabulary*. We think "pithy" is one great hot-shot word that really impresses people, unless you have a lisp. Then you seem simply vulgar. On second thought, forget it. We're not going to give you any more good words that you'll just twist around and say, "Ha! That sounds just like...!" We'll just use some big words instead and then you won't know what the hell we're talking about. Oops. We mean: Won't know what the hell we're talking about, huh?

Anyway, to return to our former discussion, everyone will assume there is some very pithy saying that is apropos. (We *warned* you.) Maybe there is. Who knows? This works great unless you're talking to someone who happens to speak German or French or Japanese and who says something to you that just might be a question. In that case, you respond with one of the following:

- Is that supposed to be Italian?

- I speak only *classical* Latin.

- I'm not sure you meant what you just said, but if so, yes, it *does* take a lot of boxes of Jell-O to fill a bathtub and, no, I *don't* want to see your mole.

- I'm rubber and you're glue. Whatever you say bounces off moi and sticks to vous.

The Opera

No, we are not talking about daytime television dramas with writers who probably get a big, fat bonus every time they have a character say, "I'm pregnant!" And we're not talking about the big ol' stage in Nashville featuring country-western stars who pull down several million dollars every year and say, "Shoot, Ah'm jist lahk you and ever'body else. 'Cept Ah pull down sev'ral million dollars ever' yeah."

No. We mean the sleep-inducing music featured on older cartoons starring Bugs Bunny and Elmer Fudd. Like when Elmer sings, "Kill da wabbit...." Very few people know anything at all about opera. Here is a handy fact that will put you light-years ahead of all your family and friends: Wagner's *Ring Cycle* is some old, gory, big-deal, 3,000-part opera, *not* a setting on a washing machine. And a lot of it is sung to the tune of "Kill da Wabbit."

Extra Credit

Memorize this. It's a translation of all the parts of Wagner's *Der Ring des Nibelungen* ("This Ring is for Nibbling On").

1. "Das Rheingold" ("Like a Rheingold Cowboy").

2. "Die Walkure" ("You're Gonna Croak, Luke Skywalker").

3. "Siegfried" ("How to Cook a Sieg").

4. "Gotterdammerung" ("Climbing the Corporate Ladder" – literally, "Reaching Up for the Next....").

Piano Lessons

"I've always wanted to learn to play the piano," you say, but you're a little worried that maybe you're too old now. You are. You can rent or buy a piano and sign up for expensive lessons and give it a try and then say, "To hell with this." Or, you can just say, "To hell with this."

Have you ever met anyone who learned to play the piano at The Big Four-O? We suppose there must have been someone, sometime, somewhere. And he sat down and entertained his friends with "The Blue Danube Waltz" and everyone clapped and congratulated him and thought, "What a jerk."

You don't need to spend time and money to get a reaction like that. If you just say, "I didn't take piano lessons and now I'm not going to play for you," you will get a standing ovation.

The Poets

When you were younger you thought poetry was for wimps. You were right. Poets aren't born. They're made by demented parents who give their kids god-awful names. Percy Bysshe Shelley. Need we say more? OK. Can you imagine the announcer at Soldier Field in Chicago saying, "Quarterback sack by the all-pro nose tackle: Percy. Bysshe. Shelley!"

The only good thing about poets is that they usually have some very lurid or pathetic circumstance in their lives that makes for wonderful conversation at cocktail parties or neighborhood bar-becues. While you're grilling up burgers for your Very Large Neighbor, you can say:

Speaking of the poet Percy Bysshe Shelley, did you know he was married to Mary Shelley and she wrote *Frankenstein*?

And he will go, "Yeah."

So then you can say, "Did you know he started the public televi-sion network, PBS?"

And he'll say, "Is there more coleslaw in the house?"

The Ballet

One advantage to becoming a Renaissance man or woman is that you can get so smart you can insult people without their even knowing it. A very good insult is, "You are as beautiful as a ballerina's foot."

Stupid people – in other words, anyone willing to be your friend – will think that's a big compliment. Obviously they have never seen a ballerina with her shoes and socks off. Neither have we. But it's a pretty safe bet her tootsies look like something that would disgust a marathon runner or a 126-year-old Chinese woman who had her feet bound when she was three minutes old.

Paying the Price

That is the price a ballerina must pay for her art. Art always has a price.

Take, for example, that black velvet painting of Elvis, the King, you got for nothing from that guy at work who was moving because his parole was being revoked.

It was free, but now you have relatives, neighbors, and friends trooping through your living room and pointing and laughing and saying, "He ain't dead. I know a guy who knows a lady who has a cousin who goes to beauty school with this gal who *swears* she seen him over to the 7-Eleven a coupla weeks ago."

Now you can't sleep at night. You toss and turn and wonder *which* 7-Eleven? That's the price you pay.

The Sistine Chapel

Speaking of paying...almost 500 years ago Pope Julius II (remembered for the frothy orange juice he served his guests) asked Michelangelo to paint the ceiling of the Vatican's Sistine Chapel. It took Mike four years. *Years!*

This isn't in any of the history books, but it seems pretty obvious that before Mike started slapping the paint around, the Pope must have asked, "Which is cheaper? By the hour or by the job?"

And Mike said, "Oh, it's about the same, I guess. I suppose by the hour would be a little less expensive." Four years. (He finished in 1512. The same year he turned 37.) We mention this only so you'll realize that the world is still filled with artists. The guy you just hired to paint your garage is a regular Picasso.

Chapter Eleven

Things

If there's one thing we can say about you, it's that you've accumulated a lot of stuff over the past 40 years. You deserve a lot of credit. As a matter of fact, that's how you accumulated all that stuff.

The Limit

Let's take a little time here to talk about credit. Back when you were in your early 20s – almost half a lifetime ago – a major national department store chain sent you – yes, you! – a credit card. With a $500 limit.

You snatched it up and ran down to the store and bought some bell-bottom jeans, a pound of double-dipped chocolate-covered peanuts, a mood ring, and a few other necessities, and before you knew it you had reached your credit limit.

But you really, really, really, really, really, really wanted a new turntable with an 8-track tape player, so you whined a little to some people in the credit department and, my, weren't they nice about it? They increased your limit!

This, of course, led to all the other cards you now carry in your wallet. A wad of plastic worth almost $20,000. That's right: $20,000! And, once again, you've reached your credit limit.

We mention this now because, after making the minimum monthly payment for almost two decades (roughly $2 billion), you have almost paid for those peanuts. Congratulations.

You Can Fool Some of the People All the Time

It's not that you're a sucker. No, you're an just an easy mark and a fool. Think about it: coonskin caps, Howdy Doody, hula hoops, Barbie dolls, love beads, blue jeans, tie-dyed T-shirts, the voyages of the starship *Enterprise*, world peace, Pong, VCRs, personal computers, CD players....

The marketing world has your head right in the cross hairs. These days, commercials for running shoes feature old Beatles' tunes. The Rolling Stones are pushing beer. June Cleaver makes cameo appearances in low-budget movies. A book on how to survive your 40th birthday makes references to the Beatles and the Rolling Stones and June Cleaver. It's all done just to get your money!

You don't need to buy those shoes. Or switch to that beer. Or see that movie. You *do* need to buy at least three copies of this book.

"A Fuller Fit"

Marketing people are playing you for a sap because they know you want to hang on to your youth. As if there's anything left of it at your age.

But they say, "Hey, we've got a special pair of jeans, just for you. Same great comfort and style. With a fuller fit." Sounds good, huh? Sure does. Much better than, "Designed just for you and your big old butt." Take the time to appreciate the effort they're going through just for you.

Isn't That Interesting!

One of the many advantages of living for four decades is that you begin to take more interest in a variety of topics. For instance, 20 or 25 years ago, would you have read an advertisement that offered A Sure Cure for the Ugly, Embarrassing, Disgusting Deformity Known as Cellulite? "The back of my thighs looked like Florida orange peels," a perky, 92-pound model confesses.

Or would you have paid attention to a TV commercial for a shampoo that "thickens those few wisps of hair still somehow sticking to the top of your head"?

But now...why, that stuff is fascinating!

And Your Teeth Are Falling Out

And what about gingivitis? Ginger Vitis? Was she the one in the evening gown on "Gilligan's Island"? No way. The topic is gum disease and *you have it*!

Since so many places put fluoride in the drinking water and so many people use a fluoride toothpaste, cavities are way, way down. But fortunately, just in time, dentists have discovered gum disease.

That's why there's a guy – a young guy, a guy in his late 30s – on the tube talking about it. He has a forehead that goes back to the label on his shirt collar and he says, "First my hair, now my gums." Or words to that effect. It's hard to tell. What with all his teeth falling out. And suddenly you think, "I want to keep my teeth!"

You haven't had that thought that since you were in the fourth grade and a classmate, Bobby I-shave-twice-a-day McPherson, grabbed you on the playground before school and said, "Gimme your lunch money."

Whoa! The mind can sure slip around at 40, can't it? Don't let that frighten you. It's very natural. As your brain's dying begins to accelerate, it's going to happen more frequently. You haven't thought about the fourth grade in a long, long time. Or about Senator McPherson.

A Bunch of Old People

One of the hardest parts about turning 40 is this: A whole bunch of famous singers and movie stars you liked for years and years are now old people.

(Don't even look at National Football League players if they have their helmets off. "There's 'Gramps' Johnson," the TV commentator will say. "He's one of the oldest still playing the game! Just turned 29.")

We suggest you subscribe to several trashy tabloid newspapers so you can keep up with all those Hollywood birthdays. You will be amazed at how many famous people made millions of dollars when they were in their early 20s. Back when you were trying to survive on the money you got selling your textbooks back to the college bookstore.

Take the Beatles, for example. When they took the U.S. of A. by storm, they were mighty young. Everybody's seen clips of them with Ed Sullivan. You might not be close to Ed's age – yet – but you do like his suit better than theirs. That's a *very* bad sign.

Back on Track

In the last section we wandered around quite a bit because that's the way you think these days, but we aren't going to follow your wandering thought patterns anymore.

So let's get back to the trashy tabloids and why you should subscribe to them. If you do, you can keep an eye out for stories on Rich, Famous, and Forty People who made big bucks years and years ago. And you can say, "Yes, he was extremely successful at a very young age, but I see that his new wife from Saturn was on a grapefruit diet and just gave birth to Siamese-twin English Springer Spaniel pups joined at the hip who look like Elvis and Priscilla. Boy, I'm glad I'm not rich and famous!"

The Price of Fame

You can say that again! "Yes, he was extremely successful at...." No, no, no. The part about being glad you're not rich and famous.

If you were rich and famous you'd have to worry about answering your doorbell and finding Robin "the" Leach on your front porch wanting to videotape your luxurious, opulent, decadent, high-caloric lifestyle. Which members of The General Public would then watch and dissect and comment on: "The back of her thighs look like Florida orange peels."

And there's another horrible risk involved in being Stinking Rich and Disgustingly Successful. Somebody like Dick "Dorian Gray" Clark could set you up for A Practical Joke!

"We've told Our Rich and Successful Friend that this formula will make the hair growing in his nose move to the top of his head," Young Dick will tell Ed McMahon and the viewers. "First, we convince this schmo to stuff pina colada-flavored yogurt way, way up into his sinuses. And then the fun really begins! Let's watch!"

Just think how lucky you are being a very poor nobody.

Pay Attention!

And speaking of Dave Clark…hey! Wake up! We were speaking of *Dick* Clark. You didn't even notice the switch. Another bad sign. Speaking of Dave Clark…yes, *Dave*. Speaking of Dave Clark, remember how people used to debate which group was better: the Dave Clark Five or the Beatles?

Now nobody claims to have liked the Dave Clark Five. Just like nobody ever voted for Nixon. The lesson here is that, as time goes by, you can deny your past. Deny it, hell! You can make up a whole new past! Lucky for you.

Your Annoying Habit

Speaking of the good old days, you need to be careful you don't keep up that annoying habit you've picked up recently. The one where you say, "They just don't make things like they used to! It's all junk, junk, junk. It all costs too much! And kids today! What is this country coming to? I just don't know!"

You sound just like your grandmother.

Ending On a Happy Note

Let's end on that happy note. There you were, spending all that time worrying about the fact that you were becoming your mother or father, when there was no need to be concerned. That was just a phase you were going through. A phase every-one nearing 40 goes through.

Now that you've actually hit The Big Four-O, forget about it! Now you're well on your way toward becoming your grandmother or your grandfather. The spitting image. Except that you're a tad more conservative. A bit more pessimistic. Not quite as healthy. And nowhere near as rich.

Happy Birthday.

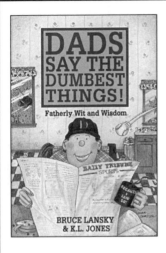

Dads Say the Dumbest Things!

by Bruce Lansky and K.L. Jones

Lansky and Jones have collected all the greatest lines dads have ever used to get kids to stop fighting in the car, feed the pet, turn off the TV while doing their homework, and get home before curfew from a date. It includes such winners as: "What do you want a pet for—you've got a sister" and "When I said 'feed the goldfish,' I didn't mean feed them to the cat." A fun gift for dad.

Order #4220

Moms Say the Funniest Things!

by Bruce Lansky

Bruce Lansky has collected all the greatest lines moms have ever used to deal with "emergencies" like getting the kids out of bed in the morning, cleaned dressed, to school, to the dinner table, undressed, and back to bed. It includes such all-time winners as: "Put on clean underwear—you never know when you'll be in an accident" and "If God had wanted you to fool around, He would have written the 'Ten Suggestions.'" A fun gift for mom.

Order # 4280

Grandma Knows Best, But No One Ever Listens!

by Mary McBride

Mary McBride offers much-needed advice for new grandmas on how to

- Show baby photos to anyone, any time
- Get out of babysitting . . . or if stuck, to housebreak the kids before they wreck the house
- Advise the daughter-in-law without being banned from her home.

The perfect gift for grandma, Phyllis Diller says it's "harder to put down than a new grandchild."
Order #4009

What's So Funny about Getting Old?

by Jane Thomas Noland
illustrated by Ed Fischer

The perfect gag birthday gift for anyone 39 and over. It's a collection of cartoons, jokes, quotes, humorous advice, anecdotes, and clues for figuring out anyone's age that will provide entertainment at any "over the hill" birthday party.
Order #4205

Familiarity Breeds Children

selected by Bruce Lansky

This collection is a treasury of the most outrageous and clever things ever said about raising children by world-class comedians and humorists including Roseanne, Erma Bombeck, Bill Cosby, Dave Barry, Mark Twain, Fran Lebowitz, and others. Filled with entertaining photographs, it makes the perfect gift for any parents you know—including yourself. Originally entitled *The Funny Side of Parenthood.*
Order #4015

Age Happens

selected by Bruce Lansky

A compilation of the funniest things ever said about growing older by the most insightful wits of all time: Ellen DeGeneris, Garrison Keillor, Bill Cosby, and many more! This book includes 15 cartoons by some of *The New Yorker's* most popular cartoonists.
Order #4025

Golf: It's Just a Game

selected by Bruce Lansky

Bruce Lansky has hit a hole-in-one with this collections of clever golf quotes from such devotees of the game as Lee Trevino, Gerald Ford, Bob Hope, and many, many more. Illustrated with some of the funniest cartoons ever to appear in *Golf Digest* and *Playboy*.
Order #4035

Are You Over the Hill?
Find Out Before It's Too Late!

by Bill Dodds
illustrated by Stephen Carpenter

Jam-packed with fun ways to remind old codgers of 34 or more that their better years are behind them. A great gag gift for friends' and family members' birthdays.
Order #4265

Also from Meadowbrook Press

✦ **The Best Baby Shower Book**
The number one baby shower planner has been updated for the new millennium. This contemporary guide for planning baby showers is full of helpful hints, recipes, decorating ideas, and activities that are fun without being juvenile.

✦ **The Best Bachelorette Party Book**
This all-inclusive book contains information on how to plan and host a great bachelorette party—plus great games, activities, and recipes. It includes the kind of spicy, fun ideas that bachelorette party-goers are looking for.

✦ **Best Party Book**
Whether it's a birthday, an anniversary, a reunion, a holiday, a retirement, shower, or the Super Bowl, this creative guide shows even the most inexperienced host how to throw a great party.

✦ **The Best Wedding Shower Book**
This revised edition offers valuable time-tested advice on how to plan and host the perfect wedding shower with great games, activities, decorations, gift ideas, and recipes.

✦ **What You Don't Know About Retirement**
"**Q**: How can I make sure my friends and family stay in touch? **A**: Move to vacation spot and live in a place with a pool. **Q**: Why is it dangerous for a retiree to miss the condo-owners association meeting? **A**: They might be elected president." Makes a great gift and provides a funny quiz to make any retirement party more fun.

We offer many more titles written to delight, inform, and entertain.
To order books with a credit card or browse our full
selection of titles, visit our web site at:

www.meadowbrookpress.com

or call toll-free to place an order, request a free catalog, or ask a question:

1-800-338-2232

Meadowbrook Press • 5451 Smetana Drive • Minnetonka, MN • 55343

THE CLEANERS ™

Written by
MARK WHEATON and
JOSHUA HALE FIALKOV

Art by
RAHSAN EKEDAL

Colors by
JON GRAEF

Letters by
MICHAEL DAVID THOMAS

NERS™

ABSENT BODIES

DARK HORSE BOOKS®

Editor
SHAWNA GORE

Assistant Editor
JEMIAH JEFFERSON

Designer
DAVID NESTELLE

Publisher
MIKE RICHARDSON

Published by Dark Horse Books
A division of Dark Horse Comics, Inc.
10956 SE Main Street
Milwaukie, OR 97222

darkhorse.com

First edition: January 2010
ISBN 978-1-59582-370-0

10 9 8 7 6 5 4 3 2 1
Printed in China

This book collects issues #1–#4 of *The Cleaners*,
published by Dark Horse Comics.

Mike Richardson
President and Publisher

Neil Hankerson
Executive Vice President

Tom Weddle
Chief Financial Officer

Randy Stradley
Vice President of Publishing

Michael Martens
Vice President of Business Development

Anita Nelson
Vice President of Marketing, Sales, and Licensing

David Scroggy
Vice President of Product Development

Dale LaFountain
Vice President of Information Technology

Darlene Vogel
Director of Purchasing

Ken Lizzi
General Counsel

Davey Estrada
Editorial Director

Scott Allie
Senior Managing Editor

Chris Warner
Senior Books Editor

Diana Schutz
Executive Editor

Cary Grazzini
Director of Design and Production

Lia Ribacchi
Art Director

Cara Niece
Director of Scheduling

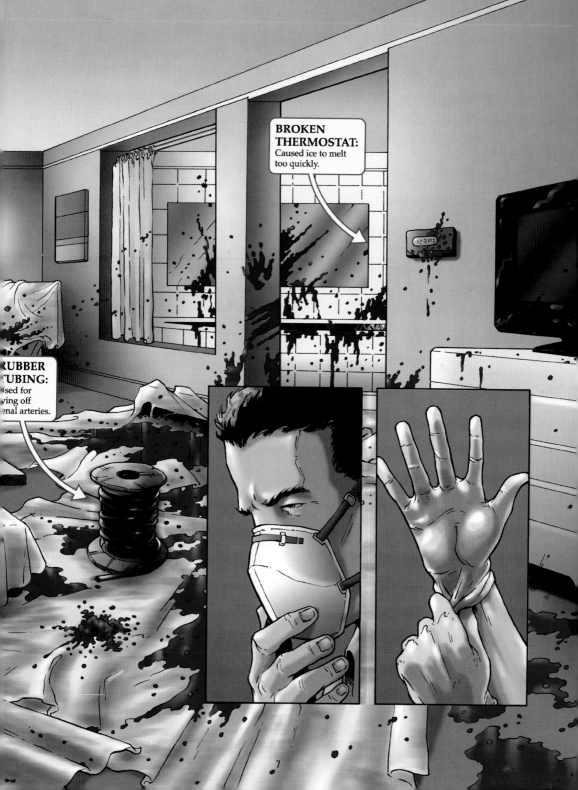

WE'RE FIXING THE A/C NOW. THE SMELL SHOULD BE GONE SOON...

YOU DON'T WANT TO DO THAT.

WHY NOT?

IF EITHER OF YOUR "GUESTS" WERE CARRIERS OF MENINGITIS OR LEGIONNAIRE'S -- THEN THEIR BLOOD ASPIRATING UP INTO YOUR VENTS AND BEING INHALED BY SOMEONE ELSE...

...MEANS A FAT LAWSUIT AGAINST YOUR HOTEL.

AND I'D EXPECT THAT'S WHAT YOU'RE SPECIFICALLY PAYING MY COMPANY TO AVOID, CORRECT?

AB... ABSOLUTELY, MR. BELLARMINE.

THE OFFICER IN CHARGE WAS WHO -- HENDERSON? WALKER?

TALBOTT. I THINK. HE WAS HERE YESTERDAY.

HIS CSI GUYS PROBABLY FOUND PLENTY LIKE IT, BUT JUST IN CASE...

I DON'T WANT TO PRESSURE YOU, BUT WE WERE REALLY HOPING TO GET THE USE OF THIS ROOM BACK BY THE WEEKEND.

THE VMAs ARE IN TOWN AND ONE OF THE LABELS BOUGHT UP ALL THE SUITES FOR AN AFTER-PARTY...

WELL, SIR -- I CAN PRETTY MUCH MAKE YOU A GUARANTEE.

IF YOU CAN KEEP THE BLOGOSPHERE AT BAY AND THE PAPARAZZI OFF THE FLOOR FOR FIVE MORE HOURS, I'LL HAVE THIS ROOM READY TO RENT BY SIX TONIGHT.

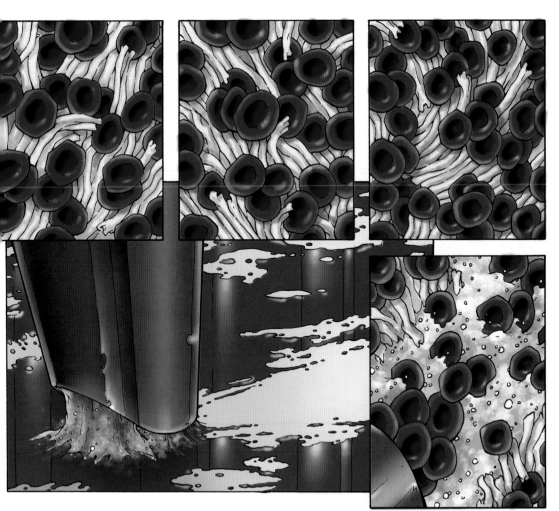

ZZZT ZZZT ZZZT

IF THAT'S HUMAN BLOOD, IT'S A BIOHAZARD. $10,000 FEDERAL FINE, YOU TRY AND CLEAN IT YOURSELF. ANOTHER TEN TO THE CITY YOU GO AND WASH IT ONTO CITY PROPERTY...

I SAID, IF THAT'S HUMAN BLOOD...

BULLSHIT. WE CALLED 911, THEY SAID *"DOG."* WE CALLED THE COPS, THEY SAID *"COYOTE."* WHATEVER IT IS, I DON'T WANT IT WITHIN TWO FEET OF WHERE MY BOY'S BEEN PLAYING ALL MORNING.

"INCONCLUSIVE" MEANS WHAT IT MEANS AND IF IT ROLLS AROUND TO "HUMAN," SIR, A JUDGE IS GOING TO SEE IT MY WAY.

SIR? IF YOU DON'T MIND ME SAYING SO, I'M THE SOLUTION HERE. YOU JUST DON'T KNOW IT YET.

RIGHT, PHIL?

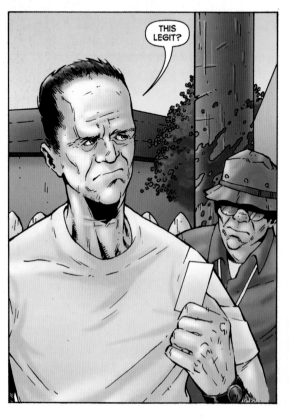

YOU KNOW WHY THEY BURY PEOPLE IN COFFINS AND AWAY FROM DRINKING WATER? BECAUSE A SINGLE HUMAN BODY IS A TOXIC CESSPOOL CAPABLE OF INCUBATING ENOUGH OF ANY GIVEN PLAGUE TO WIPE OUT A CIVILIZATION.

MY FINGER TOUCHING THIS -- IF IT REALLY IS HUMAN BLOOD -- PUTS ME AT RISK FOR HEPATITIS A & B, STAPHYLOCOCCUS, STREPTOCOCCUS, AND HIV.

IF YOU HAD TURNED YOUR HOSE ON THIS ONE FIVE-INCH PATCH AND IT DRAINED DOWN THE FENCE, INTO THE ALLEY OR WHEREVER, YOU WOULD NOW HAVE A CONTAMINATED SURFACE AREA OF ROUGHLY AN ACRE IDENTICAL TO WHAT'S NOW TRYING TO MULTIPLY AND FIND A WAY INTO MY BODY ON THE TIP OF MY FINGER.

IF YOU HAD DONE THAT TO THIS ENTIRE AREA, THAT WOULD MULTIPLY BY OVER A THOUSAND PERCENT -- HUNDREDS OF ACRES COULD BE AFFECTED. IT COULD EVEN GET IN THE DRINKING WATER.

WHAT CAN I DO?

FIRST -- HAVE A VET SHAVE YOUR DOG AND DESTROY THE HAIR.

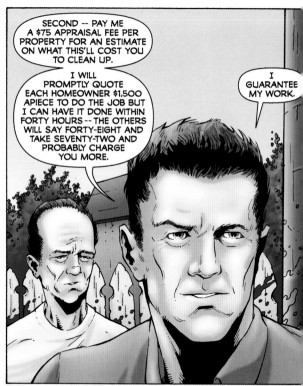

SECOND -- PAY ME A $75 APPRAISAL FEE PER PROPERTY FOR AN ESTIMATE ON WHAT THIS'LL COST YOU TO CLEAN UP.

I WILL PROMPTLY QUOTE EACH HOMEOWNER $1,500 APIECE TO DO THE JOB BUT I CAN HAVE IT DONE WITHIN FORTY HOURS -- THE OTHERS WILL SAY FORTY-EIGHT AND TAKE SEVENTY-TWO AND PROBABLY CHARGE YOU MORE.

I GUARANTEE MY WORK.

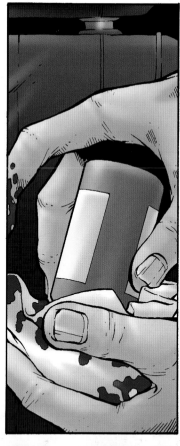

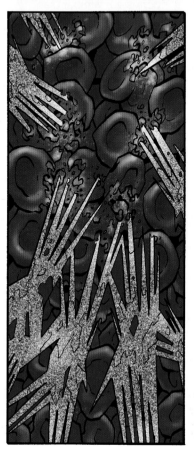

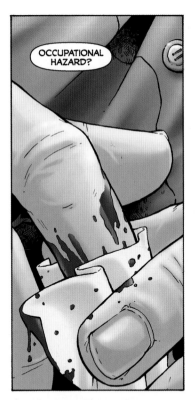

OCCUPATIONAL HAZARD?

I DON'T EVEN FEEL IT ANYMORE. JUST ONE OF THOSE THINGS.

WHAT IF IT TURNS OUT TO BE A DOG? WELL, A BIG DOG, I GUESS. DOG-S, PLURAL?

IF THERE WAS EVEN A CHANCE THIS WASN'T HUMAN, THEN THEY WOULD'VE GONE HOME. *"INCONCLUSIVE"* ALSO MEANS A POSSIBILITY OF MULTIPLE VICTIMS. BUT WITHOUT LABS, YOUR LOCAL PRECINCT CAPTAIN WON'T SIGN TO OPEN A CRIME SCENE.

MULTIPLE...?

SORRY.

NO, I APPRECIATE YOUR HONESTY.

WERE YOU REALLY A DOCTOR?

A LONG TIME AGO.

COULDN'T HACK IT, HUH?

SOME-THING LIKE THAT.

GOOD LUCK. FORTY HOURS, STARTING NOW.

ROBERT?

19

WHAT?

YOU OKAY?

THE CHECKS CLEAR ON THE SUN VALLEY CONTRACTS?

JUST NOW. YOU'RE ALL SET. PULLING AN ALL-NIGHTER?

KNUT GET BACK FROM DOWN-TOWN?

YEAH, HE'S WORKING THE BLOOD SAMPLES YOU BROUGHT BACK. IT'S MORE THAN ONE PERSON. A LOT MORE.

FIGURED. THEY GONNA DISCOVER THAT AND KICK US OUT OF THEIR ACTIVE CRIME SCENE?

NOT SO FAST. THE BLOOD'S OLD -- YEARS AND YEARS, SOME OF IT.

WHICH IS PROBABLY WHAT THE FIRST CSI TEAM ON-SITE DISCOVERED -- AND WHY THEY TURNED IT OVER TO PUBLIC WORKS.

AND WHY ANNIE THOUGHT WE MIGHT TAKE A LOOK.

WHAT DO WE HAVE, KNUT?

THE IRON AND CHLORIDE LEVELS ARE ALL OVER THE PLACE. I'M SURE SUN VALLEY PD IS THINKING LESS "MULTIPLE HOMICIDE," MORE ILLEGAL DUMPING WITH OVER 100 DIFFERENT INDIVIDUALS REPRESENTED.

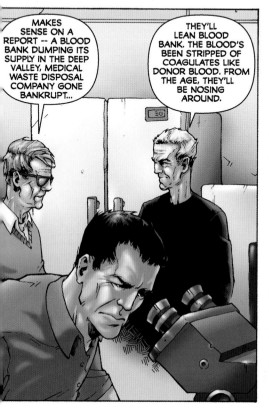

MAKES SENSE ON A REPORT -- A BLOOD BANK DUMPING ITS SUPPLY IN THE DEEP VALLEY, MEDICAL WASTE DISPOSAL COMPANY GONE BANKRUPT...

THEY'LL LEAN BLOOD BANK. THE BLOOD'S BEEN STRIPPED OF COAGULATES LIKE DONOR BLOOD. FROM THE AGE, THEY'LL BE NOSING AROUND.

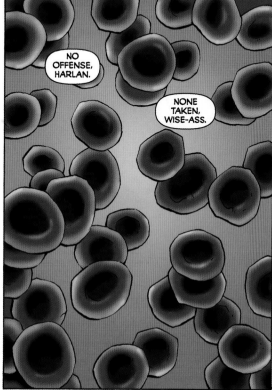

NO OFFENSE, HARLAN.

NONE TAKEN, WISE-ASS.

21

YES, SIR -- WE RESEARCHED THAT AND FOUND THAT THERE WAS A CEMETERY THERE, INCORPORATED AROUND 1909, THOUGH ONLY ABOUT SEVENTEEN BODIES WERE EVER INTERRED.

IF YOU PLAN TO BUILD THERE, YOU'LL NEED TO MAKE BEST EFFORTS TO CONTACT DESCENDANTS IF YOU WANT TO INTER THEM ELSEWHERE AND YOU ARE LIABLE FOR COSTS.

I UNDERSTAND THAT, SIR, BUT GAINING TITLE INCLUDES OWNERSHIP OF EVERYTHING BELOW THE GROUND AND, IN THIS CASE, STEWARDSHIP. IT'S YOUR RESPONS--

KLIC!

CHERYL, I'M KNOCKING OFF.

OKAY...

22

BLUE-LIGHT EMITTER: Used in concert with Luminol to reveal blood.

ELECTRIC THERMAL FOGGER: Creates "dry fog" to bring down particulates as they're stirred up.

FLUID SOLIDIFIER: Self-explanatory.

2-GALLON SPRAYER: For introducing decontaminating agents and odor counteractants to hazmat site.

MR. BELLARMINE?

MR. DE LA GARZA. GOOD EVENING.

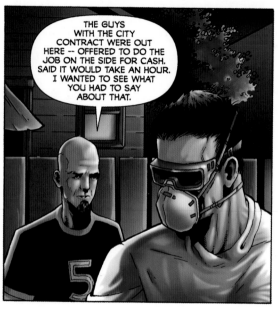

THE GUYS WITH THE CITY CONTRACT WERE OUT HERE -- OFFERED TO DO THE JOB ON THE SIDE FOR CASH. SAID IT WOULD TAKE AN HOUR. I WANTED TO SEE WHAT YOU HAD TO SAY ABOUT THAT.

THEY SCORCHED THIS, RIGHT? THEN TARRED IT?

THAT'S RIGHT.

THEN THEY POURED A CHEMICAL ON THE GRAVEL, HIT IT WITH A BLACK LIGHT, AND SCOOPED OUT ANYTHING WITH BLOOD ON IT BEFORE BLEACHING DOWN THE REST.

THAT'S IT TO A T.

SEE, THAT'S JUST SLOPPY. THE MINUTE THEY HIT THAT WITH THEIR TORCH, THE BLOOD ASHED UP INTO THE AIR AND BECAME PART OF THE LOCALIZED BREATHING ATMOSPHERE. IT'S HEAVY, SO ANY EMBERS WILL PROBABLY FALL AROUND THIS AREA.

IT'S CALLED ASPIRATION. A SOLID PARTICULATE ENTERS THE BREATHABLE AIR AND CAN INFECT A HUMAN, OR -- IN SOME CASES -- EVEN A PLANT. A PROFESSIONAL UNDERSTANDS THE IMPORTANCE OF STERILITY, ESPECIALLY AROUND BLOOD.

MAMA, MAMA... I WANT MY MAMA...

HELP ME...

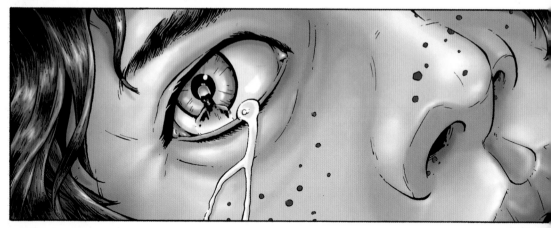

30

PLEASE...

NO SALT QUITE YET. WE MAY BE ABLE TO FINISH THIS BAG. THEN WE'LL REHYDRATE YOU...

...AND START OVER AGAIN IN THE MORNING.

≥SOB≤

≥SOB≤

≥SOB≤

ZZZT...

ZZZT...

ZZZT...

WHAT-CHA GOT, KNUT?

I STARTED MATCHING TYPES TO THE NATIONAL RUNAWAYS DATA-BASE. GUESS HOW MANY MATCHES I FOUND?

THREE OR FOUR?

ELEVEN. A PARTIAL MATCH ON SIX MORE. OLDEST DATES BACK TO 1981.

ONE MORE THING. THE BLOOD IS STILL ALIVE. IT'S SELF-SUSTAINING ON A CELLULAR LEVEL, USING ENZYMES FROM ALL DIFFERENT EXPRESSED BLOOD TYPES TO CONSTANTLY REPAIR AND RESTORE FUNCTION.

SEEMS ANNIE WAS RIGHT ABOUT THIS BEING ONE FOR US, HUH?

SOUNDS LIKE, HARLAN'S ON HIS WAY IN, BY THE WAY, SO I'LL SEND HIM OUT THERE.

THANKS. KEEP ME APPRISED.

WILL DO. BE CAREFUL.

POLAR PAK®

GOT ANY KODIAK LEFT? I'LL TAKE A SLEEVE.

I'LL HAVE TO CHECK IN BACK.

8/1 – 11/1

11/15 – 12/26

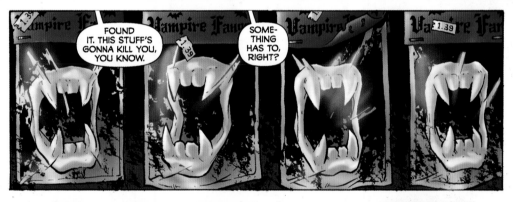

FOUND IT. THIS STUFF'S GONNA KILL YOU, YOU KNOW.

SOME-THING HAS TO, RIGHT?

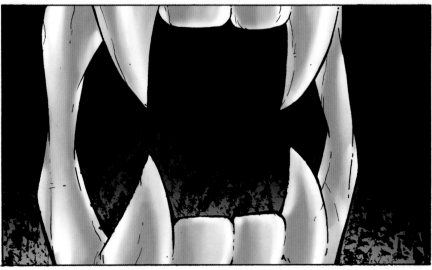

I NEED YOU TO ISOLATE THE UNMATCHED SAMPLES AND DETERMINE WHICH ARE THE MOST RECENT AND GET THOSE TO HARLAN -- PARTICULARLY ANY THAT MIGHT BE CURRENT OR POSSIBLY FROM A BODY STILL BREATHING.

YOU GOT IT.

WHERE ARE YOU OFF TO?

BACK TO THE SCENE. I'VE HAD ANNIE RUN REAL ESTATE SALES DISCLOSURES AND PRIORS OF RESIDENTS AND JUST WANT TO SEE WHAT ELSE I CAN SEE.

"GOOD LUCK WITH THAT..."

THOSE CATS STILL OUT THERE?

YEAH...

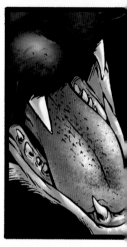

DAD SAID TO SHOO THEM AWAY BEFORE THEY PEE ON EVERYTHING.

THEY'VE BEEN LICKING, THEN PEEING A LOT, RIGHT?

YEAH, ALL OVER THE ALLEY.

THIS SHOULD FIX THAT PROBLEM.

HENRY! GET BACK IN HERE!

WHAT DID I TELL YOU ABOUT STRANGERS?

SORRY...

IT'S MY FAULT, MR. REARDON. I ASKED A...

AS YOU WERE, MR. BELLARMINE. I'LL GET TO YOU IN A SEC.

IT'S OKAY TO SCREW UP. JUST REMEMBER WHAT WE'VE TALKED ABOUT.

YES, DAD.

I THOUGHT YOU WERE FINISHED.

GETTING THERE. WANTED TO REPLACE A COUPLE OF THE FENCE POSTS.

YOU STILL HAVE ANY OF THE PAINT YOU USED ON THIS SITTING AROUND IN YOUR GARAGE?

...SO, SHE'LL TAKE HIM FOR THE MONTHS I'M HAULING CROSS-COUNTRY OR OUT ON THE RIG WHENEVER I CAN GET A ROUGHNECKIN' SHIFT --

-- BUT AFTER KATRINA, YOU'VE GOT EVERYBODY AND THEIR DOG LOOKING FOR THAT SPOT.

SORRY I GOT RILED ABOUT HENRY. THERE WAS ONE OF THOSE CHILD ABDUCTIONS A COUPLE OF NEIGHBORHOODS OVER TWO WEEKS AGO...

...A KID NAMED COOP LEWIS.

THAT'S WHY I STARTED THE NEIGHBORHOOD WATCH PROGRAM, COUPLE OF US KEEPING AN EYE OUT. ME AND MR. DE LA GARZA HAVE THIS BLOCK.

HOW'S THAT BEEN GOING?

SO FAR, SO GOOD. I'D BE LYING IF I SAID I WAS THINKING OF MUCH OTHER THAN HENRY, THOUGH.

AIN'T THAT THE DAMNEDEST THING? NEVER SEEN A CAT GO AFTER ANYTHING LIKE THAT EXCEPT ANTIFREEZE. BUT IF THAT WAS PRESTONE, THERE'D BE A MESS OF DEAD CATS OUT HERE, I'D THINK.

THEY'RE LICKING SYNTHETIC GLYCEROL BROKEN DOWN FROM EPICHLORO-HYDRIN.

SAY *THAT* THREE TIMES FAST.

IT'S LIKE AN ANTI-FREEZE, BUT CAN BE USED AS A MOISTURIZER, A SOAP, A FUEL ADDITIVE, CONVERTED TO ETHANOL, OR...

A CRYO-PROTECTANT FOR RED BLOOD CELLS. IT GETS ADDED TO DONOR BLOOD IN ORDER TO STORE IT FOR UP TO TEN YEARS.

THAT'S WHAT THE COPS WERE SAYING -- THIS WAS SOME KIND OF WASTE DUMPING.

THEN I GUESS THAT'S WHAT IT IS.

GLYCEROL

THAT'S THE END OF IT.

TELL YOUR NEIGHBORS YOU'LL BE GETTING MY INVOICE IN THE MAIL IN THE NEXT DAY OR SO.

WILL DO.

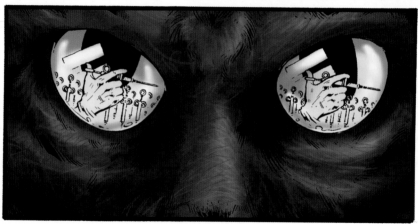

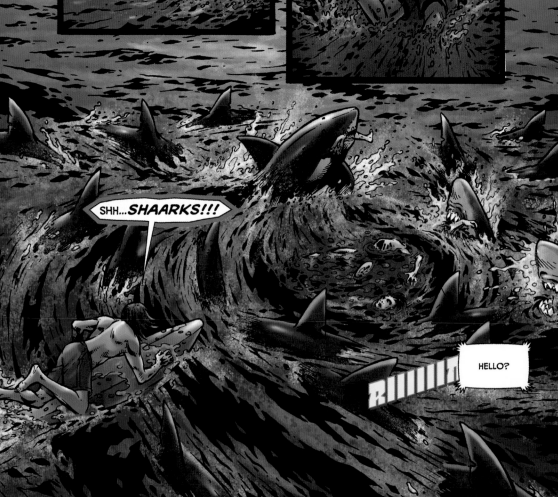

YEAH?

HARLAN -- IT'S JUNIOR CLEMENS AT THE BURBANK PRECINCT.

MORNIN', JUNIOR. WHAT CAN I DO FOR YOU?

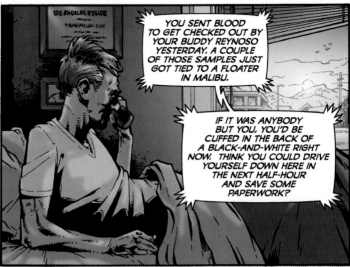

YOU SENT BLOOD TO GET CHECKED OUT BY YOUR BUDDY REYNOSO YESTERDAY. A COUPLE OF THOSE SAMPLES JUST GOT TIED TO A FLOATER IN MALIBU.

IF IT WAS ANYBODY BUT YOU, YOU'D BE CUFFED IN THE BACK OF A BLACK-AND-WHITE RIGHT NOW. THINK YOU COULD DRIVE YOURSELF DOWN HERE IN THE NEXT HALF-HOUR AND SAVE SOME PAPERWORK?

YOU GOT IT. SEE YOU IN FIFTEEN.

APPRECIATE IT.

HYDROGEN PEROXIDE

I COULD PROBABLY ORDER THIS FOR YOU IN BULK.

YOU'D MISS ME.

THAT'LL BE $13.42.

AUG California 2009
TB1-342

ONE MORE TIME?

THEY MANAGED TO GET TEN OF 'EM ON THE FLOOR OF THE FIRST AMBULANCE, BUT THERE'S A SECOND WAGON COMING...

THEY'RE COVERED WITH SAND AND NOW IT'S ALL OVER THE FLOOR IN HERE.

HOW'D THEY IDENTIFY HIM AS THE LEWIS KID SO QUICK?

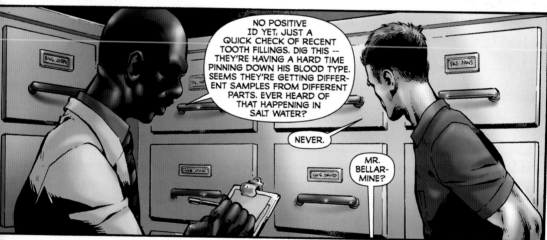

NO POSITIVE ID YET, JUST A QUICK CHECK OF RECENT TOOTH FILLINGS. DIG THIS -- THEY'RE HAVING A HARD TIME PINNING DOWN HIS BLOOD TYPE. SEEMS THEY'RE GETTING DIFFERENT SAMPLES FROM DIFFERENT PARTS. EVER HEARD OF THAT HAPPENING IN SALT WATER?

NEVER.

MR. BELLARMINE?

JUNIOR CLEMENS, BURBANK PD. I'VE GOT A FRIEND OF YOURS FILLING OUT A REPORT BACK AT MY PRECINCT. WE NEED TO TALK.

'COURSE.

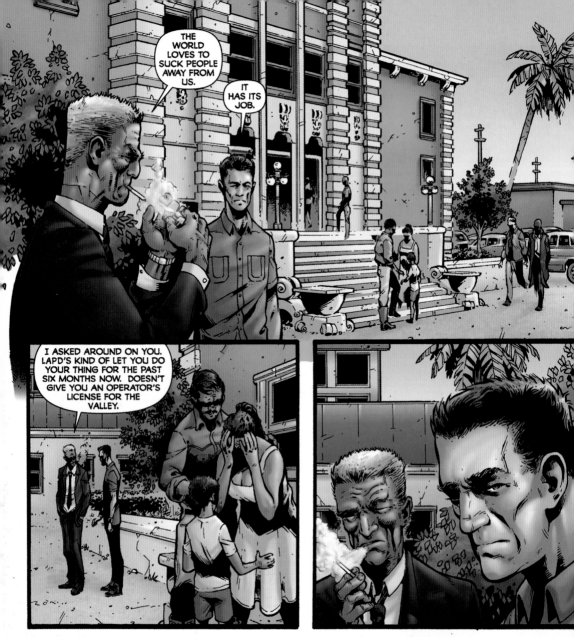

THE WORLD LOVES TO SUCK PEOPLE AWAY FROM US.

IT HAS ITS JOB.

I ASKED AROUND ON YOU. LAPD'S KIND OF LET YOU DO YOUR THING FOR THE PAST SIX MONTHS NOW. DOESN'T GIVE YOU AN OPERATOR'S LICENSE FOR THE VALLEY.

I CAN CLOSE THE BOOKS ON HARLAN. MAKE IT SO PEOPLE KNOW IF THEY'RE HELPING HIM OUT WITH LITTLE LEADS HERE AND THERE, THEY JUST GOT A CEILING BUILT OVER THEM. THIS NEEDS TO WORK BOTH WAYS. WHO KILLED THAT BOY?

IT'S A *HARVESTER.* A PERSON WHO CAN ADD YEARS ONTO THEIR LIFE BY CONSUMING THE TISSUE MATTER -- IN THIS CASE, BLOOD -- OF OTHER HUMANS. IT'S APPARENTLY BEEN SO RARE IN WORLD HISTORY THAT MOST SCIENTISTS CAN'T AGREE THAT IT EXISTS, MUCH LESS HOW IT WORKS.

YOU PIECE OF SHIT. WHAT DO YOU TAKE ME FOR?

55

WHO AND WHERE?

REARDON. AUTO ZONE. $52.45.

FUCK. GET OUT TO SUN VALLEY AS FAST AS YOU CAN. I'LL MEET YOU THERE.

I'M HEADING TO THE STORE. WANT ME TO PICK SOMETHING SPECIAL UP FOR DINNER? THERE'S A GAME ON TONIGHT. ASTROS.

BURGERS ON THE GRILL?

BURGERS ON THE GRILL. I'LL PICK UP SOME ICE CREAM, TOO.

ROCKY ROAD.

ROCKY ROAD IT IS.

SLAM!

MAZEROSKI
SEMAN

PITTSBURGH
PIRATES

toZone!

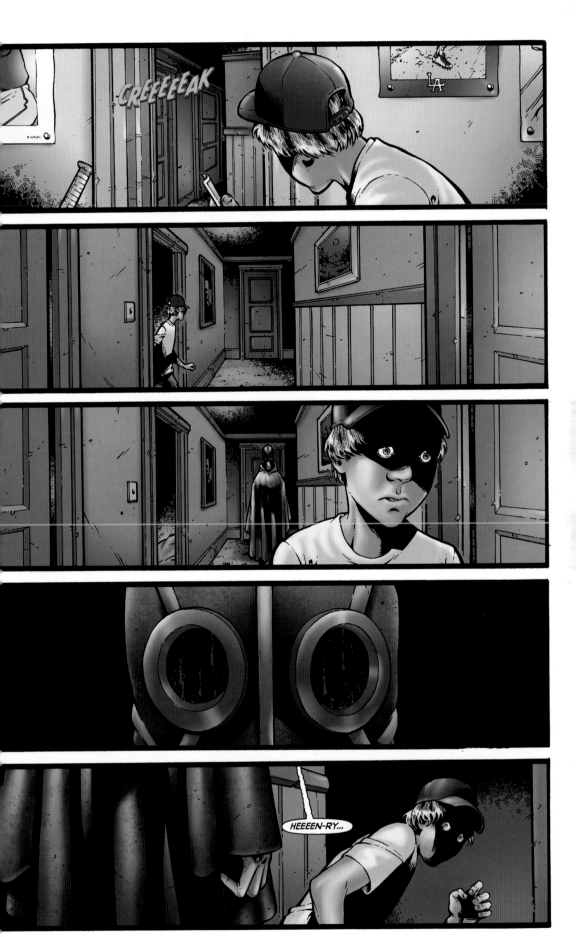

CHARCOAL
BRIQUETTES

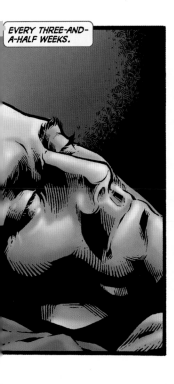

EVERY THREE-AND-A-HALF WEEKS.

...HAVE SCHEDULED A PRESS CONFERENCE FOR 10:00 THIS MORNING TO ASK THE PUBLIC FOR THEIR HELP IN PROVIDING LEADS ON THE COOP LEWIS CASE...

THE BODY OF TWELVE-YEAR-OLD COOP LEWIS WAS DISCOVERED...

MORNIN', DARLING.

GOT ME AGAIN, BABY.

KNOCK...
KNOCK...

KNOCK...
KNOCK...
KNOCK...

PITTSBURGH PIRATES

WHEN I WENT BACK OUT,
I DIDN'T SEE ANYTHING.
I HALF EXPECTED TO
FIND A DEAD DOG OR
CAT, BUT THERE WAS
NOTHING THERE.

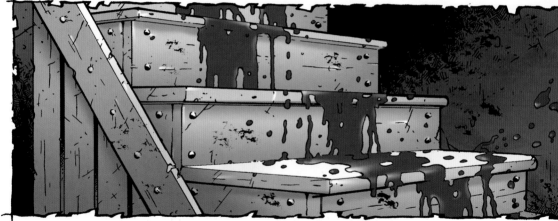

THE POLICE GAVE ME ONE OF THOSE BOXES TO PUT ON MY PHONE -- *"JUST IN CASE HE'S A RUN-AWAY."* BUT THEY'RE JUST SAYING THAT TO MAKE ME FEEL BETTER...

...RIGHT?

IT'S FOR ALL INCOMING CALLS. MIGHT BE THINKING SOMEBODY ELSE MIGHT CALL.

YOU KNOW WHO DID THIS.

YES.

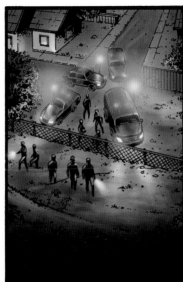

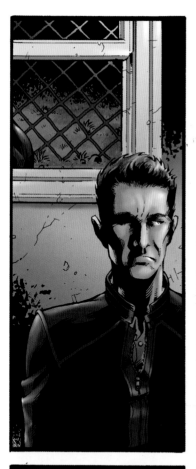

HEY, HARLAN -- YEAH. ROBERT WANTED YOU TO HEAD OUT TO SUN VALLEY. HE'S EXPECTING A LOT OF COPS ON THIS ONE. FIGURED YOU COULD HELP.

YEAH, HE KNEW I'D BEEN WORKING ROUND THE CLOCK SO HE WENT AHEAD AND GAVE ME THE NIGHT OFF.

WHAT CAN I GET FOR YOU?

TWO SIDECARS. AND IF THE BAR'S RUNNING SLOW, BRING ME A THIRD IN FIFTEEN MINUTES.

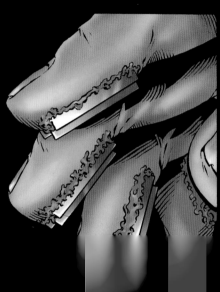

POLICE -- DON'T MOVE...

I'M UNARMED. MY NAME IS ROBERT BELL...

LIE DOWN FLAT ON YOUR STOMACH, PUT YOUR HANDS BEHIND YOUR HEAD, AND INTERLACE YOUR FINGERS.

I'VE GOT ONE SUSPECT, CAUCASIAN MALE, MID-THIRTIES...

BLAM!!

MICKEY?!

ARE YOU THE ONLY ONE IN THE HOUSE?

THAT I KNOW OF, YES. BUT THERE'S A WOMAN WHO LIVES HERE...

ALONE?

YES, BUT SHE MAY BE DANGEROUS.

WHAT'S HER NAME?

LAURA ELDRIDGE.

IF YOU'RE LYING TO ME, YOU'RE GOING TO HAVE A LOT TO ANSWER FOR.

JUST BE CAREFUL.

MICKEY?

I... I CAN'T.

WAIT -- YOU DIDN'T HEAR THE REST OF IT.

IF YOU DON'T, I WON'T KILL HENRY EITHER. INSTEAD, I'LL MAKE HIM LIKE ME. HOW LONG DO YOU THINK HE CAN SURVIVE THAT?

HOW LONG HAVE YOU?

A LONG, LONG, LONG TIME.

IT'S TOO LATE TO CHANGE YOUR MIND.

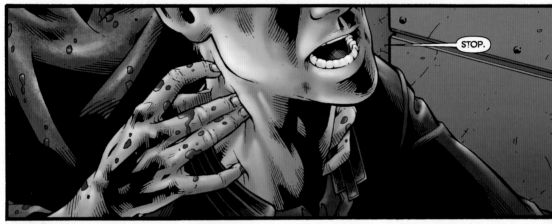

OMNIA AD DEI GLORIAM.

NO SWEAT ACE.

THERE'S NO TOUCHING THE DANCERS, SIR -- EVEN THEIR HAIR. YOU'RE GOING TO HAVE TO LEAVE.

EENIE, MEENIE, MEINE, MO...

CATCH...

...LA TIGRA...

...BY THE TOE.

IF SHE HOLLERS, LET HER GO...

93

KAFF...
KAFF...
KAFF...

HOW'D YOU GET OUT OF THERE?

MACGYVERED IT. EASIER WHEN YOU HAVE THE BLUEPRINTS OF THE HOUSE IN YOUR POCKET AND KNOW WHERE THE STORM SEWER MEETS THE PROPERTY.

YOU BRING WHAT I ASKED YOU TO?

YEAH. BUT SHE COULD BE FIFTY MILES AWAY BY NOW.

LESS THAN FIVE. AND SHE'S WAITING FOR US.

AND THE BOY?

TURNED.

WE'LL FIND HIM.

I FIRST ARRIVED IN THE
LOS ANGELES BASIN
ON JULY 28, 1882.

MY PARENTS WERE FROM
OHIO, WHERE MY GREAT-
GRANDFATHER HAD FOUGHT
IN THE OHIO VALLEY
CAMPAIGNS UNDER GEORGE
ROGERS CLARK DURING THE
AMERICAN REVOLUTION.

I WAS BORN IN 1869
AND MY PARENTS'
NAMES WERE OTIS
AND CAROLINE.

I THINK I HAD A BROTHER.

THAT'S ALL I'VE DETERMINED ABOUT MY "ROOTS" OVER THE PAST 126-127 YEARS.

I'VE FORGOTTEN EVERYTHING ELSE -- OR BLOCKED IT OUT TO KEEP MY SANITY.

THAT'S THE THING YOU LEARN VERY QUICKLY. IT'S NOT ABOUT GUARDING YOUR LIFE...

SNAP

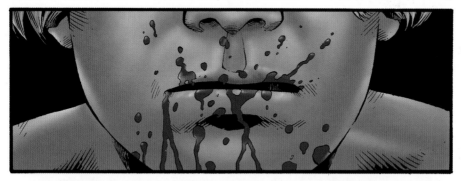

...IT'S ABOUT GUARDING YOUR MIND. DO YOU HAVE ANY IDEA HOW HARD IT IS TO KEEP FROM GOING CRAZY...

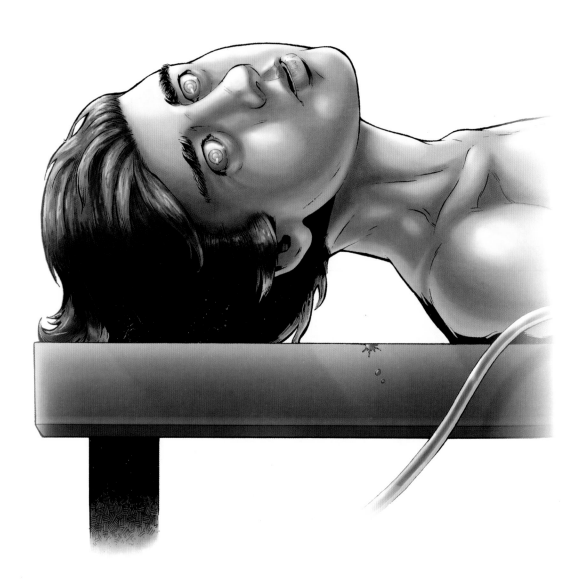

THE CLEANERS SKETCHBOOK

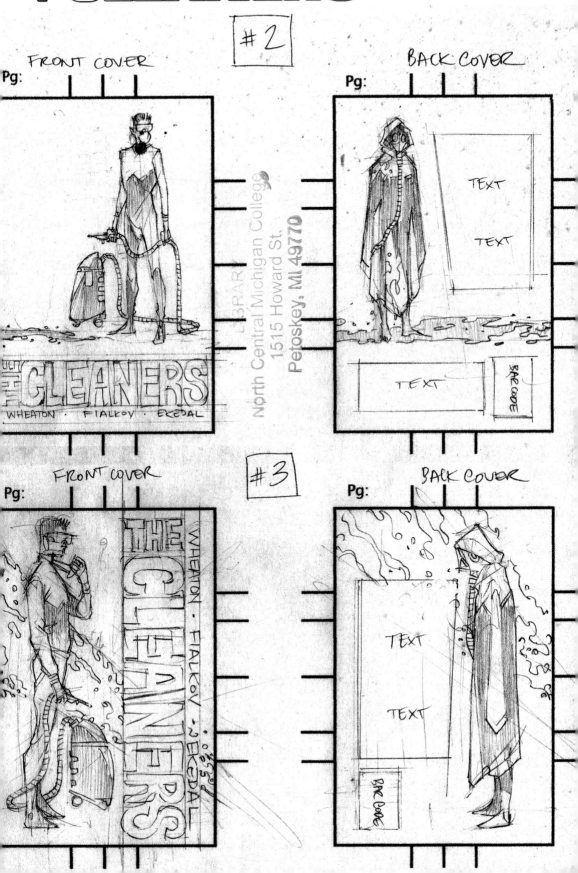

#2

FRONT COVER

Pg:

CLEANERS
WHEATON · FIALKOV · EKEDAL

BACK COVER

Pg:

TEXT

TEXT

TEXT

BARCODE

#3

FRONT COVER

Pg:

THE CLEANERS
WHEATON · FIALKOV · EKEDAL

BACK COVER

Pg:

TEXT

TEXT

BAR CODE

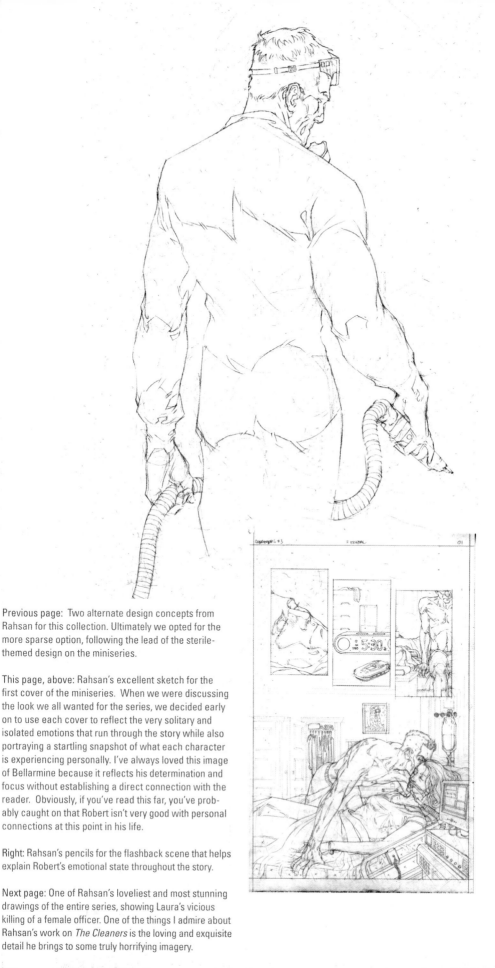

Previous page: Two alternate design concepts from Rahsan for this collection. Ultimately we opted for the more sparse option, following the lead of the sterile-themed design on the miniseries.

This page, above: Rahsan's excellent sketch for the first cover of the miniseries. When we were discussing the look we all wanted for the series, we decided early on to use each cover to reflect the very solitary and isolated emotions that run through the story while also portraying a startling snapshot of what each character is experiencing personally. I've always loved this image of Bellarmine because it reflects his determination and focus without establishing a direct connection with the reader. Obviously, if you've read this far, you've probably caught on that Robert isn't very good with personal connections at this point in his life.

Right: Rahsan's pencils for the flashback scene that helps explain Robert's emotional state throughout the story.

Next page: One of Rahsan's loveliest and most stunning drawings of the entire series, showing Laura's vicious killing of a female officer. One of the things I admire about Rahsan's work on The Cleaners is the loving and exquisite detail he brings to some truly horrifying imagery.

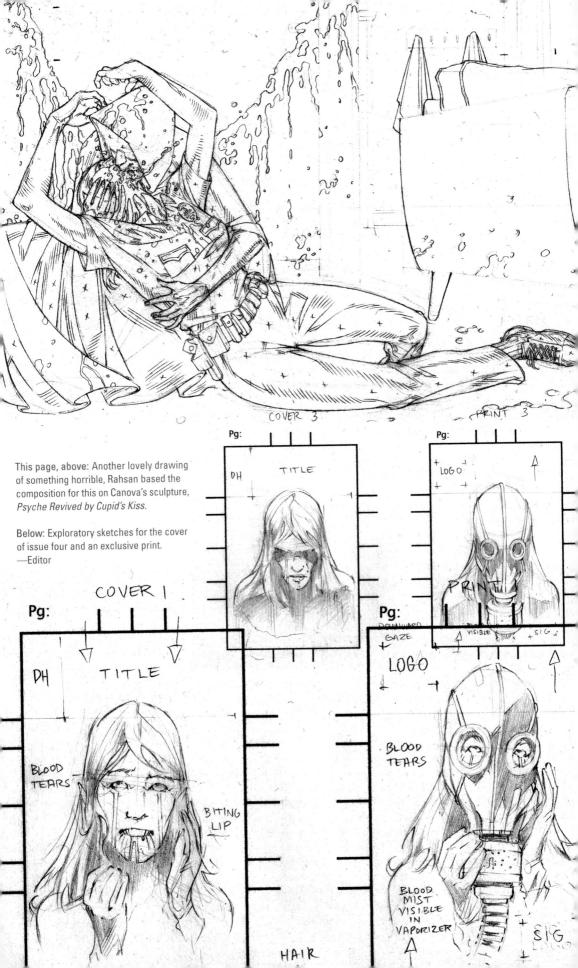

COVER 3

PRINT 3

This page, above: Another lovely drawing of something horrible, Rahsan based the composition for this on Canova's sculpture, *Psyche Revived by Cupid's Kiss.*

Below: Exploratory sketches for the cover of issue four and an exclusive print.
—Editor

Pg:

DH   TITLE

Pg:

LOGO

PRINT

DOWNWARD
GAZE   VISIBLE   SIG

COVER 1

Pg:

DH   TITLE

BLOOD
TEARS

BITING
LIP

HAIR

Pg:

LOGO

BLOOD
TEARS

BLOOD
MIST
VISIBLE
IN
VAPORIZER

SIG

ALSO FROM DARK HORSE BOOKS

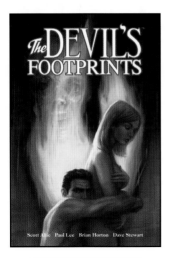

THE DEVIL'S FOOTPRINTS
Scott Allie, Paul Lee, and Brian Horton

The youngest son of a deceased sorceror, desperate to protect his family from a mysterious curse, digs into his dead father's bag of tricks. But his desire to protect his loved ones leads him to mix deception with demon conjuration, isolating himself in a terrible world where his soul hangs in the balance. "Recommended." —Alan Moore

ISBN 978-1-56971-933-6 | $14.95

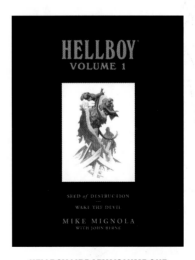

HELLBOY LIBRARY VOLUME ONE
Mike Mignola

Since Mike Mignola's *Hellboy* first hit the stands in 1993, it has become a cultural sensation, racking up a dozen Eisner Awards and inspiring numerous spinoffs. *Hellboy Library* Volume 1 collects *Seed of Destruction* and *Wake the Devil* with the original introductions by Robert Bloch and Alan Moore.

ISBN 978-1-59307-910-9 | $49.95

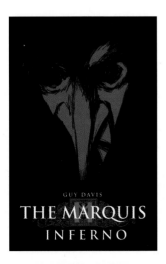

THE MARQUIS: INFERNO
Guy Davis

In eighteenth-century Venisalle, faith governs life and death, and the guilty hide their shame behind masks. It is to this stronghold of the Inquisition that the souls of hell have escaped to possess the living, spreading sin, murder, and chaos. Amid the carnage, only the Marquis is blessed with the clarity to recognize the demons—and the means to return them to Hell.

ISBN 978-1-59582-368-7 | $24.95

MYSPACE DARK HORSE PRESENTS VOLUME THREE
Various

The third volume of the online comics anthology *MySpace Dark Horse Presents* showcases Dark Horse's broad range of genres and iconic characters, including *Usagi Yojimbo*, *Buffy the Vampire Slayer*, and *Emily the Strange*, and introducing new favorites *Dr. Horrible*, *Witchfinder*, and *Achewood*!

ISBN 978-1-59582-327-4 | $19.95

DARK HORSE BOOKS®
darkhorse.com

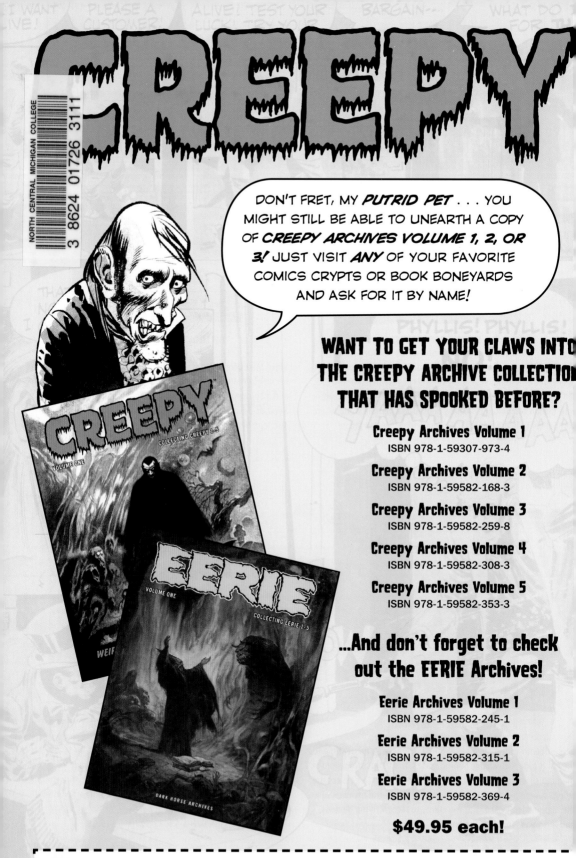